Encountering Poverty

POVERTY, INTERRUPTED

Editors

Ananya Roy, Luskin School of Public Affairs, University of California, Los Angeles
Clare Talwalker, International and Area Studies, University of California, Berkeley

Editorial Board

Vincanne Adams, Medical Anthropology, University of California, San Francisco
Alain de Janvry, Agricultural and Resource Economics, University of California, Berkeley
Victoria Lawson, Geography, University of Washington, Seattle
Bill Maurer, Anthropology, University of California, Irvine
Raka Ray, Sociology, University of California, Berkeley
Eric Sheppard, Geography, University of California, Los Angeles
Laura Tyson, Business Administration and Economics, University of California, Berkeley

Poverty, Interrupted serves as a platform for public scholarship on poverty, inequality, and poverty action. Launched at a historical moment of acute inequalities across and within the global North and global South, the series foregrounds research, analysis, and theory that interrupt mainstream frames of wealth and poverty. In doing so, it presents established and emerging scholars and activists with new pedagogies and practices of inhabiting and transforming an unequal world, while at the same time interrogating how poverty has emerged as the dominant analytic for reflecting on social differences.

Encountering Poverty

THINKING AND ACTING IN AN UNEQUAL WORLD

Ananya Roy,
Genevieve Negrón-Gonzales,
Kweku Opoku-Agyemang,
and Clare Talwalker

With illustrations by Abby VanMuijen

UNIVERSITY OF CALIFORNIA PRESS

University of California Press, one of the most distinguished university presses in the United States, enriches lives around the world by advancing scholarship in the humanities, social sciences, and natural sciences. Its activities are supported by the UC Press Foundation and by philanthropic contributions from individuals and institutions. For more information, visit www.ucpress.edu.

University of California Press
Oakland, California

© 2016 by The Regents of the University of California

Library of Congress Cataloging-in-Publication Data

Roy, Ananya, author.
   Encountering poverty : thinking and acting in an unequal world / Ananya Roy, Genevieve Negrón-Gonzales, Kweku Opoku-Agyemang, Clare Talwalker.
      pages   cm.— (Poverty, Interrupted ; [2])
   Includes bibliographical references and index.
   ISBN 978-0-520-27790-8 (cloth : alk. paper)
   ISBN 978-0-520-27791-5 (pbk. : alk. paper)
   ISBN 978-0-520-96273-6 (ebook)
   1. Poverty.   2. Poverty—Research.   I. Negrón-Gonzales, Genevieve, 1978– author.   II. Opoku-Agyemang, Kweku, author.   III. Talwalker, Clare Vineeta, 1967– author.   IV. Title.
   HC79.P6R687   2016
   362.5—dc23

                                                                  2015031936

Manufactured in the United States of America

24   23   22   21   20   19   18   17   16
10   9   8   7   6   5   4   3   2   1

In keeping with a commitment to support environmentally responsible and sustainable printing practices, UC Press has printed this book on Natures Natural, a fiber that contains 30% post-consumer waste and meets the minimum requirements of ANSI/NISO Z39.48-1992 (R 1997) (*Permanence of Paper*).

The publisher gratefully acknowledges the generous support of the Anne G. Lipow Endowment Fund for Social Justice and Human Rights of the University of California Press Foundation, which was established by Stephen M. Silberstein.

Contents

1 Introducing Poverty

Ananya Roy, Genevieve Negrón-Gonzales,
Kweku Opoku-Agyemang, and Clare Talwalker

STARTING POINTS

In 2007, the University of California, Berkeley, undertook an unusual endeavor: it launched a new undergraduate minor in Global Poverty and Practice. Almost immediately, the program started to grow rapidly, drawing students from a wide range of majors and featuring classes with enrollments big enough to fill the campus's largest classrooms. The expansive scope of the program was perhaps most evident in its curriculum, which reached beyond the traditional social sciences, integrating material from diverse disciplines such as engineering, public health, and business. Despite its academic success, the Global Poverty and Practice Minor marked a departure from the normal format of the university's undergraduate curriculum. From the start, it aligned itself with students who were interested in troubling the divide between theory and practice, refusing to relegate the work they did in organizations and communities to the second-class status of extra-curricular activity. Instead, the program was inspired by the energy of a generation of students passionate about poverty action and intent on transforming an unequal world. The Global Poverty and Practice Minor was also unusual because, while it was housed

1

in a powerful and prestigious institution, it did not promote the conceits of a stereotypical global university. Students in the program were not meant to be vanguards of social change; they were not billed as global leaders; they were not given the charge to solve urgent human problems. Instead, they were invited to work modestly, reflexively, and persistently within both marginalized communities and communities of inquiry.

The starting point for *Encountering Poverty* is the collective labor that we—and many others who are not a formal part of this publication—put into creating and guiding this program. In the book, we share the analytical frameworks and methodological principles that underpin the Global Poverty and Practice Minor, not because they constitute a blueprint for an ideal curriculum or a handbook for poverty action but rather because they are a starting point for a new field of inquiry: critical poverty studies. Our premise is that the conceptual and pedagogical dilemmas faced by the program illuminate the debates and struggles currently being waged in the broad ambit of poverty knowledge and poverty action. Take the case of the following three dilemmas that recur throughout this book.

- Poverty has become a dominant analytic for understanding social difference. Yet this analytic tends to rely on categories such as "poor others" or "global poor" that obscure the histories and social relations of impoverishment. In this way, poverty experts and poverty actors come to believe that they can help poor others or eradicate global poverty, but rarely do they acknowledge how they are a part of the systems and processes that produce and reproduce poverty—that poverty is not inevitable but actively constructed. This also means that they are comfortable relying on those very systems and processes, with just a bit of repurposing, to mitigate poverty. Philanthrocapitalism and ethical consumerism are only two of many possible examples of poverty action that relies on the same forms of wealth and types of global markets that produce impoverishment. This topic is complicated, and entire careers— academic and professional—are made through studying and acting on poverty.

- As the global university gears up to find "real-world solutions to poverty"—a tag line that, for a while, was used by the Blum Center for Developing Economies, where our program is partly housed at the University of California, Berkeley—it draws on disciplines that promise to provide the tools for such solutions or, at the very least, knowledge about the lives of the poor. But these disciplines—engineering, *denouncing other fields*

economics, public health, urban planning, architecture, anthropology, education—have a long history of failed interventions in the problem of poverty. In some cases, they are even implicated in producing and deepening poverty, due to roots that stretch back to colonial administration and rule. Yet, somehow, there is faith that this moment of poverty knowledge and poverty action will be different. *We do bes*

- Activated in the context of a digitally interconnected world, the problem of poverty is of global scope and concern. Across great distances, it makes visible the plight of the poor, motivating self-styled global citizens to take action. But these global citizens, poised to act, are usually located in the global North. From their dispersed efforts to the "real-world solutions" launched by global universities, today's poverty action seeks to spread ideas and interventions from the West to the Rest. Writing of an earlier moment in development, anthropologist Arturo Escobar describes this process as an "enframing" of the non-Western world through tropes of "poverty and backwardness" (1995, 7). Escobar's *Encountering Development* is an important starting point for this book. But at least three vectors clash and collide with the efforts to solve Third World problems with First World benevolence and big ideas. The first is the renewal and reinvention of development in and by countries of the global South. The second is the globally interconnected poor people's movements that cut across North and South. The third is the persistence of poverty, especially racialized poverty, in the prosperous countries of the global North. If this racialized poverty is seen not as an anomaly but as a necessary supplement to wealth, then the dilemma of poverty action is even more daunting.

Critical poverty studies, as we have conceptualized it, takes the (seemingly solvable) problem of poverty as its starting point. But it uses the dilemmas generated by this proposition, such as those outlined above, to stage a conceptual and pedagogical shift. In particular, it foregrounds social relations of impoverishment, a historical understanding of development, and a reflexive approach to action. While it takes these dilemmas seriously, however, critical poverty studies is not paralyzed by them but rather views them as occasions for creating frames of thinking and acting in a highly unequal world.

This, we believe, is the role of critique in relation to the problem of poverty and the aspirations of poverty action. The practice of critique requires that we subject everything, including our desire to do good and our urge to act, to unrelenting scrutiny. Nothing is sacred. None of us can claim innocence. None of us can hide behind good intentions. Yet critique is also always the search for alternatives, an impulse akin to the motto "another world is possible," which has attended so many of the anticorporate globalization movements. Put another way, this book is premised on the argument that it is through the patient work of critical theory that we can sustain thoughtful and meaningful social change. However, to do so requires interrupting dominant frames of global poverty that present poverty as a problem to be solved through immediate action. Indeed, this is the mandate of the book series in which this book appears, Poverty, Interrupted. We borrow the idea of interruption from two texts of critical theory: Nancy Fraser's *Justice Interruptus: Critical Reflections on the "Postsocialist" Condition* and Vinay Gidwani's *Capital, Interrupted: Agrarian Development and the Politics of Work in India.* Gidwani (2008, 218) interrupts conventional accounts of capitalism by devoting attention to "regions of life," such as "culture" and "nature," that are not fully assimilated into capital's restless movement. He thus provides us with a critical understanding of capitalism that allows us to imagine ideas and practices "beyond capital's reach." Fraser (2007, 3) writes that amid "resurgent economic liberalism," when "egalitarian commitments appear to recede, a globalizing wall-to-wall capitalism is increasingly marketizing social relations, eroding social protections, and worsening the life-chances of billions." But it is from this location that she insists upon conceiving "provisional alternatives to the present order that could supply a basis for progressive politics" (Fraser 2007, 4).

CONTACT ZONES

We undertake the work of critical poverty studies in this book by examining three encounters with poverty. First, in seeking to understand the global context of the discovery and visibility of poverty, we focus on how college students and young professionals—who are part of a generation dubbed "millennials," a term especially common in the global North—encounter and seek to help "poor others." They are the foot soldiers in the proliferating global campaigns to end poverty; they are the ubiquitous presence in the global conscience that is marshaled to attend to each new global crisis, each new human disaster. We argue that new scripts for global citizenship and personhood are being negotiated at the site of such encounters. We also argue that this newly articulated and young global citizenry must be seen as a new type of poverty expert, one that is producing distinctive forms of poverty knowledge in the crucible of volunteerism, charity, aid advocacy, and humanitarian engagement.

Second, we foreground the encounter between systems of knowledge and the problem of poverty. Accompanying the prominence of global poverty are new types of intervention and new methodologies of assessment and evaluation. No longer consigned to the realm of social work or sociological investigation, poverty is being refashioned in engineering labs and through microeconomic field experiments. What is of interest to us in this book is that the study of global poverty entails a breadth of disciplines and professions that far exceeds the traditional work of development. A new knowledge landscape is in the making. Business schools are embarking on global social venture competitions, fields such as "poor economics" and "development engineering" have been formulated, the field of "public health" has been recalibrated as "global health," and centers and programs concerned with information and communication technologies for development have been launched. On the one hand, the question of poverty is reshaping powerful disciplines and professions, from economics to engineering. On the other hand, the conceptualization of poverty is being profoundly determined by the involvement of such disciplines and their worldviews.

In the encounter between knowledge and poverty, we highlight another plot line, one that challenges the reframing of poverty in the dominant languages of science and economics. The poverty concept itself, we note, is today most robustly claimed by governments, banks, development practitioners, development economists, and the founders and employees of international organizations. It delineates a community upon which to act, and it appears to justify such action. The alternative plot line we highlight is the importance of exploring—as an anthropologist might—how the poverty framework is a construct, one that is not always aligned with the social experiences of the people who are deemed poor but is always productive, generating its truth claims, its institutions, and its accompanying sets of practices. Critical poverty studies thus foregrounds both the

multiple frameworks that people deemed poor employ themselves in acting and making sense of their lives and the work that the poverty concept
does in the world.

Third, we situate such encounters with poverty in the historical
context of development, which we understand to be both an ideology and
project of human progress achieved through economic growth. Our title
draws inspiration from Escobar's landmark 1995 book, *Encountering
Development: The Making and Unmaking of the Third World*, in which
he presents the idea and practice of development as a Western project
imposed on the societies of Asia, Africa, and Latin America during the
post–World War II period. These societies were diagnosed as poor and
backward, and development sought to spread "indubitable models" of
prosperity and modernity from the West to the Rest (Escobar 1995, vii).
The contemporary encounter with poverty, we argue, emerges from this
history of development, which is itself in a new and confounding phase
with the emergence of developing nations in the global South and of globally interconnected poor people's movements. To encounter poverty today,
we contend, we must reckon with this history as well as with these emer-
gent forces. Such a reckoning is vitally important for critical poverty
studies.

For us, each of these three encounters with poverty is a terrain of contestation, sometimes with the potential to imagine and create alternatives.
None is fixed in its enlistment. None is rigid in its meaning. Following
geographers Victoria Lawson and Sarah Elwood (2014, 211), we seek to
uncover and foreground the critical junctures at which encounters with
poverty become "contact zones," "boundary-breaking, transformative
moments" that "lead to new negotiations of identity, privilege, political
responsibility and alliance." Thus, as we discuss poverty action, we are
keenly aware that eager global citizens from the North travel to the South
seeking to solve the problem of poverty, thereby rehearsing an old colonial-
ity of power in a newly configured global order. Yet we are also attentive to
how such action stirs up self-doubt and self-critique, which can lead college students to reject "voluntourism" and enlist them in struggles against
the forms of neoliberalization that are deepening poverty as well as
enmeshing them in debt. Similarly, we explore how a powerful discipline
such as economics, long entangled with the project of development, seeks

to rationalize poverty expertise through models and metrics. Economics wields considerable influence because of its use of models, which can provide an abstract depiction of human behavior. But the encounter between the discipline of economics and the problem of poverty stirs up questions that cannot be fully addressed by these models and metrics. As evident in welfare economics (for example, the work of Amartya Sen), or in the new economics of inequality (for example, the work of Thomas Piketty), such questions remind us that economics has its origins in moral philosophy. Political economy, which now seems to be a separate discipline, was in fact the domain of economics, such that a discussion of the allocation of resources was also a discussion of the power-laden distribution of resources. Moral philosophy has come to be obscured in contemporary economics, but the problem of poverty might just force a return to these original questions.

Once again, this is the important work of critique. We critically examine the relationship between our home disciplines—in economics, anthropology, education, and urban planning—and the problem of poverty. Take, for example, the field of education, which conceives of itself as being uniquely positioned to tackle poverty. The discipline views poverty as a structural condition that impacts students' lives, constrains their learning, and shapes their educational outcomes. In this conceptualization, the school is a site of possibility, the location within which lives can be improved. Whether schooling is in fact effective at lifting individuals "out" of impoverished conditions is not the question—there is evidence that this has happened and does happen. However, a vast body of scholarship also points to the role schools play in the social reproduction of inequality and to the history of schooling as tied to policing and the maintenance of social class, and there is clear empirical evidence of schools acting as a sorting mechanism, preparing the rich and the poor to take on their respective roles in the economic life of society. How can this be reconciled with the idea that the right combination of resources, policy priorities, and effective techniques will be enough to "lift" individuals out of poverty and that the cumulative effect of this will alter the economic landscape?

When our Global Poverty and Practice students are confronted with this contradiction, they are forced to contend not just with the "conditions" of injustice and inequality in schooling but also with the roots of those conditions. It is a moment in which their understanding of education shifts from believing in the power of an institution whose potential has not yet been realized because of structural constraints to understanding that these constraints are engineered, crafted, and designed in accordance with the broader social order. We ask them if they are familiar with the language around "failing schools," and there is always a chorus of agreement; they see information about this on the news, read about it in articles, and hear about it in their education classes. Perhaps more significantly, it resonates with what they have seen in their own lives—young people with enormous potential who fall through the cracks. They have been taught to approach this conundrum with the belief that the educational system is failing and that it is doing so because there are not enough resources provided to schools. At this point, we pose to our students a different set of questions: What if we consider the opposite? What if we were to consider the possibility that the education system is not failing but rather is working exactly the way it was intended to? What if we entertain the idea that the difference between schools in wealthy communities and schools in poor communities and the differential outcomes for wealthy students and poor students is by design? It is a moment of reckoning because it not only shakes the foundation of a system they believe in but also forces them to reconsider their own location within it, calling out the structures of meritocracy, credentialism, and success. It is from within this moment of profound discomfort that we insist on challenging systems of education and their designed reproduction of inequality.

COLLECTIVE LABOR, PLURAL AUDIENCES

Who we are and where we come from is an important part of how we, the four authors of this book, have conceptualized our approach to critical poverty studies and how we teach and share our organizing frameworks for it. We are a Ghanaian political economist of development, an Indian-born anthropologist of the Indian public and of global volunteerism, a critical urban studies scholar who was born in India and later became an American, and a Chicana scholar of political activism and undocumented migrant students. We come from diverse fields, draw on divergent disciplinary and methodological training, and make our intellectual home in different spaces in the academy. However, our work is bound by shared theoretical commitments and genealogies of thought. Specifically, our version of critical poverty studies is rooted in an understanding of the development of capitalism as a global economic system. Using the economy as a focal point of analysis does not presuppose a reductionist approach that renders social struggle, civil society, or resistance to a subjugated status. Instead, we situate the production and protection of global capitalism as an ongoing process, one that is continually being contested and remade. This articulation forges a direct link not only to the colonial histories and anticolonial struggles of our collective recent past but also to the civil rights movement and the ongoing struggles for economic and social justice led by grassroots groups in the United States and across the globe. Embedded in this analytical trajectory, then, is a theory of change that contests the idea that justice can be legislated through the courts or won at the ballot box, that poverty can be alleviated once we discover the right technological fix or the correct social intervention, and that inequality can be mitigated by the integration of the poor into the global marketplace through selling their labor power, selling their goods, or becoming indebted.

Above all, we come to this book as teachers. Our students are coming of age politically in a moment that is marked by a coalescence around neoliberal sensibilities and market fundamentalism that portrays their massive student debt as the logical and commonsensical price of being educated, that situates the market as uniquely capable of fixing the problem of poverty, and that is wary of aid, welfare, and "handouts" (unless the recipients are the capitalist elite). This moment, however, is also marked by the fundamental failure of the capitalist state to protect its most marginalized subjects. In North America, it is the moment of Trayvon Martin, Michael Brown, Eric Garner, and Freddie Gray. It is the moment of massive fee hikes at public universities across the country, including at the University of California, Berkeley, the very institution at which this project was born. It is the moment of the disappeared students of Ayotzinapa in Mexico. Yet it is also a moment marked by mass social unrest and grassroots activism that is fighting back against these attacks and demanding that the state be held accountable. It is within such contradictions that we find our students negotiating power and privilege. These students represent the possibility of an alternative future, but a critical piece of that potential lies in making a clear, unequivocal connection to the genealogies of thought that are outlined here. The pull to eliminate poverty is not only insufficient but also misguided unless the attempts to do so are rooted in analysis that acknowledges that poverty is an integral part of the growth of capitalism, that it is mapped onto colonial histories, and that it is connected to global social movements.

This book is our effort to share collective and ongoing poverty studies scholarship with plural audiences: college students, high school and university teachers, scholars of development, development professionals, social justice advocates, and many more. To students, we offer a book that takes seriously their aspirations to create a better and more just world but that also insists that existing frameworks cannot be simply repurposed to accomplish such goals. In the same way that one cannot successfully hammer a round peg into a square hole, trying to make old frameworks act in new ways will not yield the progress we strive for. Critical poverty studies, we hope, will allow students to learn about—and act on—the histories, institutional arrangements, and structural conditions that have created poverty. However, this book is not a workbook, nor is it a field manual or a blueprint. It provides a methodology and pedagogy for critical thinking and transformative action, one where doubt and contradiction rather than certainty are seen to be generative of social change. The analytical starting point for this inquiry centers the (dis)juncture between theory and action rather than treating it as peripheral; a praxis-based pedagogy grounded in an analysis of wealth and inequality reminds us that building a field of inquiry also relies on a kind of public intellectualism which prioritizes teaching and learning. Through the vector of praxis, we push back against both anti-intellectualism and obscure theorizing.

Our use of the term "student" includes those who are no longer enrolled at colleges and universities. This takes into account all of the young people who are finding their way in the field of poverty studies—as teachers, nonprofit workers, community organizers, advocates, and practitioners—who no longer have student IDs but who still desire to maintain an engagement with learning. They tell us that they want to bring theory to bear on their hard work on the ground and that they are hungry for a way to inhabit and transform an unequal world. This book is an invitation to them as well.

Our book also speaks directly to teachers and scholars because we engage a crucial question facing higher education today: How can curricula remain relevant to society and prepare students to grapple with the world's problems? Educators will find that *Encountering Poverty* does more than simply provide the kind of historical background, conceptual understandings, and description of skills required to conceptualize poverty and inequality in interdisciplinary and transdisciplinary ways. In this book, as we have done in our Global Poverty and Practice curriculum, we consider how public health might benefit from sociology, how anthropology raises useful questions for public policy, and how the professional schools invite historians and social critics of all kinds to apply themselves to the problems of the day. It is as important for a public health educator to question the modern forms of governance and management of society that are endemic in poverty reduction strategies as it is for anthropologists to ask how their forms and subjects of study might be usefully applied to an existing poverty intervention or state welfare program. Thus the questions that we raise are ones that can and should be raised in any discipline and across many disciplines. Our students are hungry for smart and conscientious ways to live and be in the world. To this end, we bring to our pages the work of scholars who are applying their critiques to real life, writing of "real utopias," as sociologist Erik Olin Wright (2010) describes them, of experiments in city planning, of livelihood generation, and of cooperative living. Telling stories of such experiments is vitally important as a counternarrative—counterpropaganda, we might say—to the "market fundamentalism," to use Joseph Stiglitz's (2002, 36) provocative phrase, of our times.

Finally, we hope that this book will also be of interest to policymakers and development professionals. As we recognize the aspirations of young global citizens, we distinguish the personal and professional aspirations of those enlisted in the institutionalized work of making and implementing policy. We are certain that they face considerable uncertainty, doubt, contradiction, and ambivalence in their lines of work, that they struggle with the sorts of puzzles and dilemmas that we outline throughout this book, and that they constantly negotiate the boundaries of privilege and social class as they act on poverty. Above all, they know that expertise is a political, not just technical, process, one in which the safety net of abstract models and metrics does not easily hold. This book makes explicit the politics of knowledge that inevitably accompanies the practice of development. It is not just that policymakers need more answers to their questions or that they need better ways of answering their questions but that, most of all, they urgently need a unified way to ask the right questions and to be comfortable with the discomfort those questions provoke. Although policymakers are classically and deservedly trained to minimize policy uncertainty, they need not look very far to understand why our proposal is critically important. The global poor face crucial dilemmas daily—such as how they will survive and live to see another day—and on some level, their questioning never truly ends. Certainty is thus a luxury that policymakers will have to sacrifice. A critical step to reconciling the mindsets of the global poor and policymakers, then, is reimagining and reconstructing economic thinking—the bread and butter of most policymakers—as dilemma-driven narratives that empower authoritative policy specialists to discover strengths in their own limits. Embracing dilemmas as a way of thinking and acting against poverty is a complementary yet distinctive way to bring experts, organizations, and institutions closer to the people they seek to serve.

A MAP OF THE BOOK

Encountering Poverty provides the conceptual and pedagogical frameworks for a field of inquiry that we are calling critical poverty studies. In doing so, what we have most relied upon is the Global Poverty and Practice Minor at the University of California, Berkeley. Our examples are drawn as much from our experiences in creating the curriculum and teaching the classes for this program as they are from our research and scholarship. It is possible to think about these examples as an ethnographic account of teaching. We hope that this ethnographic voice provides a fine texture to our analysis. However, we also recognize that, like all ethnographic narratives, ours is fraught with problems of representation. Thus, in discussing specific interactions with our students, we not only disguise various markers of identification but also create composites so that an individual stu-

dent would not recognize herself or himself in the story. We have also borrowed from each other's experiences in a writing process that has been iterative and shared. With this in mind, we often use "we." Sometimes, when an experience pertains only to one of us or when the details are uniquely biographical, we speak in the first person. By using this collective voice, we hope to have conveyed a sense of the collaborative labor that we have valued so much while retaining the distinctive disciplines and worldviews we each bring to this shared work.

The book's second chapter, written by Ananya Roy, elaborates on the various meanings of "encountering poverty" that anchor this book. She focuses on how, in an age of digitally visible poverty, college students and young development and advocacy professionals create a sense of self through encounters with poverty, both spatially distant poverty and spatially proximate poverty. It is often in and through such encounters that they negotiate the boundaries of social class, make sense of the global economy, articulate theories of social change, and even produce poverty expertise. She asks whether such encounters also carry the possibility of understanding and acting upon social relations of impoverishment. Neither denigrating nor celebrating different types of poverty action, she highlights both the aspirations and the self-critiques advanced by millennials. Such encounters with poverty must be understood in their historical context, and Roy analyzes that historical context as an age of poverty, one in which global development institutions have taken up the problem of poverty as something to be solved. Drawing on the legacies of development studies, she interprets the age of poverty as a new moment in a long history of development interventions. This moment, which she describes as a rearranged world, is one in which geographies of prosperity and sovereignty are being redrawn across North and South. This global order, no longer that of Bretton Woods, necessitates a rethinking of poverty knowledge and poverty action. Roy suggests that globally interconnected social movements have already initiated such critical thinking, drawing attention to the predations of financialization and corporate globalization and imagining alternative institutional arrangements.

In the third chapter, "Governing Poverty," Roy returns to discourses of development and their framing of the problem of global poverty. Focusing on the iconic debate between economists Jeffrey Sachs and William Easterly about the causes of and remedies for poverty, she examines how college students respond to the recurring frame of market failure versus state failure. But both Sachs and Easterly, she argues, pin their hopes on the ineluctable sweep of economic growth and democratic transformation. In doing so, they elide what she calls the "puzzles of poverty"—the relationship between capitalism and poverty and between colonialism and (under)development. Stepping outside the frames of this debate, she insists, is vitally important if we are to understand how poverty is produced and how and why it persists in a world of prosperity. For this, she turns to three problem spaces of poverty actions, each of which amplify the challenges of thinking wholly within economic liberalism and its assumptions of opportunity and equality: microfinance, post-disaster rebuilding, and urban social movements. In each of these problem spaces she highlights ways of thinking and acting that challenge social relations of impoverishment and that view poverty as more than merely the lack of economic and technological resources.

The master painter and physician of market society, of course, is the discipline of economics, and that is what Kweku Opoku-Agyemang discusses in the fourth chapter, "Modeling Poverty." Economics, he argues, is on a quest for answers about how to solve global poverty. In particular, economists seek out solutions that are definitive, verifiable, and certain. In turn, the effectiveness of policy makers and development professionals depends heavily on these aspirations. Perhaps because of this single-mindedness, economics has repeatedly turned to the science of evaluation to tackle questions of global poverty. Given its influence, this is not an approach or a language that invites one to tarry with it, and yet this is just what Opoku-Agyemang does in his portrayal of economics as a series of dilemma tales. The format of dilemma tales, he suggests, is used in Ghana and other African countries to present children with logical and philosophical questions. The goal of these tales is not to pinpoint a correct answer. Rather, their aim is to replace the search for answers or action blueprints with the refinement of human debate about a reality that can never be perfectly modeled but at best only approximated with useful insight. So it is and should be with economics as well, Opoku-Agyemang suggests. Writing as a development economist, he notes that it is necessary to admit that there are more questions than answers about global poverty. For example, what *is* global poverty? He argues that economists know less about how to engage this question than they would like to admit. This is partly because global poverty as a lived experience is so much more than the lack of economic and social resources. It is very hard to succinctly state what "being poor" is, what it means and does to a human being, without sacrificing much of the meaning of the term. This uncertainty though, he argues, is something all economists must become more comfortable with. Opoku-Agyemang thus promotes a critical, humanist, storytelling approach, fully cognizant that this might cost the sense of certainty that science has comforted economists with for so long. To understand global poverty from an economic standpoint, he contends that a dilemma-based approach has much to offer policy makers, development professionals, and even economists.

While the first few chapters describe and diagnose key and dominant approaches to understanding today's poverty and inequality, the final two chapters reach for alternatives. In chapter 5, "Fixing Poverty," Clare

Talwalker notes that the battle to end poverty often seems to be stuck in a rut. Capitalism produces wealth but also inequality. The modern nation-state puts out a partial safety net for some, thereby supporting capitalist growth, notwithstanding its accompanying inequalities. Therefore, much of where capital goes and what capital does on the global stage is out of its control. In this chapter, Talwalker uses the term "utilitarian" to refer to the range of current attempts to grapple with poverty and inequality, all of which assume and are contained by the particular interplay of the market and the nation-state in liberal societies, an interplay to which there is widely assumed to be no alternative. But simply fiddling around with the inevitable interplay of market and state for any society is stifling, unsatisfying, and frustrating, and demands precisely a search for alternatives. As its particular contribution to critical poverty studies, Talwalker's chapter marks this longing for an alternative—a longing that we know is out there today in so many places around the world and, we think, also in the hearts and minds of the readers of this book. It is an inchoate longing—perhaps deliberately so. Noting, as philosopher Charles Taylor did, that it was the Romantics that answered back to nineteenth century utilitarianism, "Fixing Poverty" is partly a call to consider the Romantic critique again to see what solutions it might be able to offer for our current concerns with poverty and inequality. Can it offer anything at all? Yet, informed by the various post-Marxist writings of Erik Olin Wright and J. K. Gibson-Graham, the chapter is also a celebration of ongoing attempts to challenge the liberal tradition, pressing up against its limits through documenting and analyzing different existing experiments by people and communities around the world who are reaching for alternative economic forms and political arrangements.

In the sixth and final chapter, "Teaching Poverty," Genevieve Negrón-Gonzales circles back to the beginning of our project with an analysis of pedagogy, since it was the navigation of the complexities of teaching a new generation of poverty actors that provided the impetus for this book. Thinking through the Global Poverty and Practice Minor as a pedagogical example foregrounds our efforts to forge a relationship between theory and action, specifically through a praxis-based pedagogy grounded in an analysis of wealth and inequality. This praxis-based pedagogy, which is concerned with the production of inequality and not just with the "alleviation" of poverty, embeds critical poverty studies in the legacy of anticolonial struggles, the civil rights movement, and struggles for racial justice in marginalized communities. It is our assertion that academic work must remain connected to grassroots struggles to end inequality and that the cultivation of poverty actors armed with critical-thinking skills is a vital part of that process. In the chapter, Negrón-Gonzales resists the idea that the aim of such inquiry or cultivation is the production of a blueprint or a plan. Instead, drawing on the pedagogical relationship with our students and an acknowledgement of the neoliberal context within which they are both configured and also configuring, she invites an engagement with ambiguity, uncertainty, and complexity. In particular, she situates praxis-based pedagogy amid the tangled dialectics of wealth, inequality, poverty, capital, and power. She asks: How can we use these imperfect spaces as locations to wage the ongoing struggle against injustice? She notes that this also means that we must train our focus on the very institution from within which we launch such questions. How do we contend with the neoliberalization of higher education, not as inevitable in a moment marked by fiscal austerity and the death of the "public," but as a project that was constructed and thus can be dismantled? This, for us, is a broader message—that systems of entrenched power are necessarily incomplete and often contain within them the space for resistance.

THE POLITICS OF LOCATION

Students arrive in our classrooms asking: *How do we end poverty?* We honor that desire, and we admire that aspiration. But, through our teaching, we shift their question to the following: *How is poverty produced, and why does it persist?* We then invite them to ask: *How are wealth, power, and privilege produced and reproduced?* This book outlines how we make this shift and why such shifts are the first steps toward the field of inquiry that we call critical poverty studies.

But all inquiry is located in, and all questions are asked from, a place on the map. We place the impulse of our students to do good and to empower the poor within the long histories of colonialism, imperialism, and development. For us, this often means turning the gaze of our students from poor others in the global South to inequality in the global North. We do so by reminding them, and ourselves, that there is nothing inherently virtuous about fighting for a living wage in Berkeley, planting community gardens in Richmond, or providing legal aid to undocumented immigrants in Oakland—all of these places are cities that constitute the "backyard" of our global university. These practices require reflexivity; they require an awareness of our "politics of location." Our attention to the politics of location is inspired by feminist poet Adrienne Rich's (1984, 210–231) essay "Notes toward a Politics of Location," in which she articulates the paradoxes of the location that is the United States: prosperity with persistent poverty, democracy with enduring racialized exclusions, an immigrant country with militarized borders. In a poem titled "Hunger," dedicated to Audre Lorde, which we read to our students on the first day of our Global Poverty class, Adrienne Rich (2002, 134–136) writes: "I choke on the taste of bread in North America / but the taste of hunger in North America / is poisoning me. Yes I'm alive to write these words." It is from this deeply contradictory location that we present this book.

But our location is not just North America, it is also the global university. We care to transform teaching and learning because we believe that the university is a terrain of social change, a place where ideas are debated and from where authoritative knowledge is produced and disseminated. It is not easy to create new communities of critical inquiry within the global university. Increasingly neoliberalized, often enslaved to the interests of the powerful, and inherently conservative in its approach to curriculum, the university can be a gated, even walled, space. Forms of knowledge that have chiseled away at these walls, those that have trespassed these gates, find themselves always facing the threat of retrenchment. Some of us four authors of this book have first-hand experience with the barricades and occupations that have sought to protect programs and pedagogies against closure and enclosure. Indeed, we present the Global Poverty and Practice Minor itself as an inherently fragile entity. With one foot in the Blum Center for Developing Economies, which is an enclave of private wealth amid the austerity of the public university, and the other foot in the university's International and Area Studies Program, which faces ongoing structural adjustment by the university, our program is both an expression and a defiance of the neoliberal university.

It is from this deeply contradictory location that we educate our students to consider how they can interrupt the ways in which the university acts on the problem of poverty—how they can speak back to their disciplines and professions. A poignant example comes from one of the first students to complete the Global Poverty and Practice Minor, Emma Shaw Crane. When she graduated from the University of California, Berkeley, in 2009, Emma was the recipient of the University Medal, the highest academic honor conferred on a graduating senior. At her commencement speech in the hallowed Greek Theater of Berkeley, Emma spoke back to the university and acknowledged her politics of location:

> It is a gorgeous day. I am so very proud. I am also heartbroken. I am heartbroken because, for me, attending UC Berkeley was to live devastating contradictions. The week I received this award, two young men I knew were shot and killed a few miles from this campus where, because they were Black and poor, they lived a world apart. Their names were Larry and Maurice. Their murders hardly made the news because, in this country, there is nothing uncommon about the unnecessary death of young African American men. I celebrated this honor knowing their families were drowning in grief.

Emma's unconventional commencement speech went on to highlight her practice experience for the Global Poverty and Practice Minor, which she completed at a continuation high school diploma program for students deemed at risk of not completing their education. The young men that she worked with, who were mostly Black, would never enroll in a four-year college or university. Less than a mile from Emma's classrooms at UC Berkeley, this was a world apart. Emma, an intellectual partner in the writing of this book, describes the Global Poverty and Practice Minor as permission to speak about that apartness. We hope that this book will similarly grant permission to see and name the worlds apart through which global poverty is constituted, lived, and regulated. We also hope that the book will serve as permission to transform the university and similar knowledge-producing institutions, along with their annals of poverty expertise and formats of poverty action.

2 Encountering Poverty

Ananya Roy

GLOBAL CITIZENS

I don't remember the first time I saw a homeless person
You can't find one of those in Lexington, Massachusetts
Birthplace of the American Revolution
Red pavement without payment of litter,
Elegant boutiques, dainty planted trees
Cul-de-sacs curled around mansions
Little girls boys bright, bubbled futures—so few chills
For want is no friend to upper middle class glut
Fear does not feed on green pesticide-not-quite-grass
As dreams are blown from mouths like bubbles—fragile, wet, still steaming
Weightless they cling to skin, nesting, become another skin, home
My home
But if you can't find a home here, then you have no home
This town is not for the homeless.

So when I came to Berkeley, I soberly took it in
Bodies line Telegraph
Like graphs of skin
Sliced off but never sewn back . . . to bodies, now so blackened
Why do I carry on my back
A wardrobe of clothes,

Sewn with hopes
Bubbling, bursting into fruits
Coating skin—sticky, sweet
I am educated.
3 university semesters,
84,297 dollars
Not so public education—

When they carry deprivation
Stigma
You are an enigma.
Our endless streaming bubbled eyes
Popping out of 'worthy' minds
Rushing on to any place but your own
Is this more bona fide? Or is it just bones?

Is this just ordinary? Can I not do anything?
Should I not look? Too uncomfortable, helpless, cynical, or just four minutes
    late to my sociology midterm?
Me, me, me.

Written by Sarah Emily Macklis, a student at the University of California, Berkeley, this poignant poem narrates the anguish of encounters with poverty. A spoken word artist and sociology major, Sarah is one of hundreds of students who flock each year to the Global Poverty course, eager to learn about poverty and inequality, as well as about ways to end poverty. They are part of the millennial generation and have grown up with an awareness of poverty alleviation. From service-learning spring breaks in faraway, impoverished villages to web-based donation systems that allow them to sponsor hungry children on a distant continent, these students boast engagements with poverty action that make for impressive resumes of volunteerism and philanthropy. They are the foot soldiers of global poverty campaigns with scopes that transcend national borders, and they enthusiastically respond to calls issued by celebrity do-gooders to save Africa, end human trafficking, build schools worldwide, and spread good sanitation to all. Distant poverty, now made visible through glossy magazine spreads, heart-wrenching television stories, and instant and constant photographs disseminated by social media, is the crucible in which millennials—college students and young professionals in the global North and global South—are making their place in the world. And an entire proliferating industry

Figure 2.1. Promotional poster for the 2014 Global Citizen Festival. (Image courtesy of www.globalcitizen.org.)

has made poverty action quite easy, albeit expensive, to undertake. As a young American, if you (or your parents) have $6,000 to spend and six weeks in the summer to spare, you can improve education for children in India, support those affected with HIV/AIDS in South Africa, or assist with the care of poor infants in Brazil. In doing so, you can, as many of the advertising slogans of the organizations that offer these experiences declare, "change their world and change yours."

What is in the making is a distinctive model of global citizenship, one animated by the impulse to take action and solve poverty. One example of such a model comes from the New York–based Global Poverty Project, whose Global Citizen Festival in Central Park, headlined by rock stars, enlists millennials in the "movement to end extreme poverty" (figure 2.1). As described in the project's Global Citizen Manifesto, at work is the imagination of collective humanity, one in which extreme poverty is "an affront to our common humanity and dignity" and where global citizens commit to a "long and hard" path to end extreme poverty "forever by 2030" (Global Citizen 2015). It is through such portals that ambitious global mandates, for example, the Millennium Development Goals and the Sustainable Development Goals of the United Nations, become an intimate part of the everyday lives of millennials.

Central to such models of global citizenship is a theory of change, one that views poverty as a problem that can be solved through the grassroots advocacy of ordinary individuals who can mobilize as global citizens: "We

1. Join the movement, become a Global Citizen. **2.** Help end extreme poverty and earn points. **3.** Choose a reward close to you. **4.** Use your points. **5.** Tickets for you and a friend.

Figure 2.2. The rewards of being a global citizen. (Image courtesy of www.globalcitizen.org.)

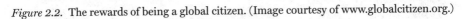

believe that the world can bring about the end of extreme poverty by 2030. It won't be quick, and it certainly won't be easy, but it can happen if we—as global citizens—create an unstoppable movement committed to changing the systems and structures that keep people trapped in extreme poverty" (Global Citizen 2015). Also central is the promise of calculable and visible impact: "Global Citizen Festival 2013 saw 250,000 people take 900,000 actions on issues of Global Health, Universal Education, Women's Equality and Global Partnerships. These actions led to 25 policy and financial commitments being made towards ending extreme poverty by 2030" (Global Poverty Project 2013). Such mobilization hinges on the vital role of social media in creating networks of global citizens drawn together by the cause of poverty alleviation. Most of all, such models of global citizenship, be they expressed through volunteerism or grassroots advocacy, reward poverty action (figure 2.2). The rewards are not simply global calculations beautifully presented in impact reports and impressive numbers but also personal rewards, from concert tickets to that priceless photograph with smiling and grateful poor children. In this way, poverty at a distance—geographically and epistemologically—becomes near. This is vitally important. But in this way, poverty also perhaps becomes a problem that can be solved, with little pain, sacrifice, and discomfort for the benevolent classes who have taken up the cause of poverty alleviation. This is vexing.

Sarah's poem bears none of the comforts of global citizenship. Her encounter with poverty expresses little certainty about problems that can be solved. Instead, it manifests a raw discomfort. Her writings can be seen as indicative of a growing self-critique of poverty action being advanced by college students and young development and advocacy professionals. This includes harsh indictments of "voluntourism," as are leveled in the much-circulated article "#Instagramming Africa," which draws attention, with considerable self-deprecation, to the common tropes of representation at work in overseas do-gooderism: "The Suffering Other, The Self-Directed Samaritan, and The Overseas Selfie." The essay ends with this advice: "I hope my fellow students think critically about what they are doing and why before they sign up for a short-term global volunteer experience. And if they do go, it is my hope that they might think with some degree of narrative humility about how to de-center themselves from the Western savior narrative. Most importantly, I hope they leave their iPhones at home" (Kascak and Dasgupta 2014). But also present in many of these self-critiques is a distinction between poverty action "here" and "there." In an opinion piece published in the *San Francisco Chronicle*, Brenna Alexander, a student in the Global Poverty and Practice Minor at the University of California, Berkeley, contrasts her experiences volunteering in an orphanage in Cambodia and at a health clinic for the homeless in the San Francisco Bay Area. She concludes: "When you volunteer at home, you encounter the injustice that resides within your own community—injustices that may collapse long-held notions and the allure of simple solutions" (Alexander 2014). The closing lines of Sarah's poem remind us of how difficult this encounter with injustice might be: "Should I not look? Too uncomfortable, helpless, cynical, or just four minutes late to my sociology midterm?"

Sarah's poem was written in response to a discussion she had with fellow students in the Global Poverty course about a literary classic, Charles Baudelaire's prose poem "The Eyes of the Poor" ([1869] 1970, 52–53). It describes a "dazzling" café on a new boulevard of "unfinished splendors" in the heart of the modern city. In it sit a pair of lovers, sharing their thoughts and dreams amidst the "expanse of mirrors," "the gold cornices and moldings," "piles of fruits, pates and game"—a cornucopia of "gluttony." Suddenly, on the street directly in front of them, appears a man of "about forty, with tired face and greying beard." With him are two children. They are all "in rags." As they stare at the café with "admiration," their eyes seem to say: "How beautiful it is! All the gold of the poor world must have found its way onto those walls." Their eyes also say: "But it is a house where only people who are not like us can go." Confronted with the "family of eyes," the man at the table in the cafe is ashamed of the "glasses and decanters" that sit before him, "too big" for the pair's thirst. But his lover wants the family banished from the street: "Those people are insufferable with their great saucer eyes. Can't you tell the proprietor to send them away?"

Written in 1869 and set against the backdrop of the sweeping transformation of Paris, "The Eyes of the Poor" presents the modern city as a space of encounters with poverty. In a city of revolution, where barricades were repeatedly raised in fights for political freedom and economic justice, the new boulevards were meant to quell revolt, remove the working classes and the poor from the heart of the city, facilitate the efficient circulation of goods and people, and foster a culture of leisure and consumption for the wealthy. But such modernization generated its own contradictions, not the least of which was the haunting presence of the poor.

In a beautiful exposition of Baudelaire's poem, philosopher Marshall Berman (1982, 153) writes: "The boulevards, blasting great holes through the poorest neighborhoods, enable the poor to walk through the holes and out of their ravaged neighborhoods, to discover for the first time what the rest of their city and the rest of life is like. And as they see, they are seen." Baudelaire takes us one step further. It is not just that the new boulevard is strewn with the rubble of displacement or that the dazzling lights of the new café make visible the eyes of the poor, but also that the encounter with poverty divides lovers and wrenches the soul. "The manifestation of class divisions in the modern city opens up new divisions within the modern self" (Berman 1982, 153). Baudelaire's poem concludes with the line: "So you see how difficult it is to understand one another, my dear angel, how incommunicable thought is, even between two people in love." In the modern city, the eyes of the poor render love itself incommunicable.

"The Eyes of the Poor" bears uncanny resemblance to contemporary times. Today, amidst the "unfinished splendors" of economic globalization, poverty is once again visible. While Baudelaire's poem signals the persistent and visible presence of the poor in a modern city redeveloped for the consuming classes, today's visible poverty is staged on a global scale. But students such as Sarah read the poem as a reminder of the immediacy of poverty, of the sharp discomfort of inequality, and of the torn and divided modern self. They thus write of the homeless bodies they must step over as they rush to their classes on progressive topics such as Global Poverty, Wealth and Inequality, Urban Social Movements. They write of their own hopes and ask: "Can I not do anything?"

THE AGE OF POVERTY

We start this chapter with Sarah's poem and the conversation it stages with a literary classic from over a century and a half ago because its aspirations and dilemmas provide a useful introduction to the study and pedagogy of global poverty.

The emergence of poverty as a public concern of global scale is one of the defining features of the end of the twentieth century and the start of the new millennium. Describing the Industrial Revolution and its social transformations, the political economist Karl Polanyi ([1944] 2001, 89) writes, "it was in relation to the problem of poverty that people began to explore the meaning of life in a complex society." So is the case today. Yet there is one key difference. The poverty of which Polanyi writes was proximate, located in the geographic immediacy of the parish, village, neighborhood, and city. The contemporary discovery of poverty is taking place in the context of unprecedented globalization. It is thus mediated by institutions of global governance (take, for example, the United Nations and its Sustainable Development Goals), situated within the context of global trade and consumption (take, for example, campaigns of responsible consumerism and fair trade that seek to remedy the injustices of economic globalization), and facilitated by new forms of global connectivity (take, for example, virtual vectors of communication and the expansion of overseas travel, including by the middle classes of the global South and North). This book is concerned with the global context of the discovery and visibility of poverty and the types of poverty action engendered by the problem of global poverty.

We are particularly interested in how the problem of global poverty is entangled with the making, and unmaking, of new models of global citizenship. What are the ways in which those empowered to imagine themselves as global citizens seek to end poverty? Of course, poverty experts—the scholars, technicians, and professionals charged with the task of diagnosing and alleviating poverty—have long acted on the problem of poverty. From economists to engineers, anthropologists to doctors, they are once again, in the age of global poverty, being mobilized to develop scientific knowledge and technical solutions. This book pays close attention to the encounter between these disciplines and the problem of global poverty, noting the long histories of seemingly new paradigms and methodologies. But another type of poverty expert abounds today: the global citizen. It is through the global citizen that poverty action becomes intimate and ubiquitous, no longer solely the work of professionals but rather everyone's work. No longer confined to the edifices of development such as the World Bank, poverty knowledge is now common sense, showing up in TED talks and popular books sold at airport bookstores. We thus pay close attention to this intimacy and ubiquity in order to understand how the problem of global poverty comes to be known, debated, and acted upon by experts as well as by the broader realm of global citizens. In doing so, we also examine the dominant forms of poverty knowledge that are being generated in the crucible of global citizenship and how they replicate, or depart from, existing modes of poverty expertise.

If poverty experts have often understood the problem of poverty as a technical one that demands analysis, measurement, solution, and impact evaluation, the mobilization of global citizens frames global poverty as a matter of conscience, personal responsibility, and ethical choices. We thus study how the emergence of poverty as a global issue has gone hand in hand with the emergence of an ethics of "extended responsibility." We borrow this phrase from Doreen Massey, a feminist geographer, who notes that the prosperity of centers of globalization—London is her particular case of inquiry—depends on distant hinterlands of labor and resources. Massey (2007, 181) argues that "ordinary Londoners, as well as the significantly wealthy, share in the responsibilities imposed by this identity." With this in mind, she calls for a consideration of "spatially distant neighbors," those at a distance but whose toil and suffering must be understood through the common humanity of neighborliness. Such transnational ethical frameworks are of vital importance in an unequal world. But the challenge of these global times, as evident in Sarah's self-critique, is also the persistent invisibility of proximate poverty. Is global poverty only a problem elsewhere, in the exotic and distant places of the world? In relation to Massey's conceptual framework, we can consider the global poor as constituted not only of spatially distant neighbors but also of spatially proximate strangers. This is the provocation posed by Baudelaire's poetry when read in today's age of global poverty. The "insufferable" family in rags at the edge of the dazzling café is the spatially proximate stranger of the modern city.

The #GlobalPOV Project, *Who Sees Poverty?*
www.youtube.com/watch?v=Xg0MgrF_DLs

In this book, we study how global citizens and poverty experts tackle global poverty not only as a geographically distant problem but also as a spatially proximate reality. Following the work of geographers Victoria Lawson and Sarah Elwood (2014), who have recently launched the Relational Poverty research network, we seek to understand how such middle-class actors encounter "poor others" and whether such encounters can trouble and rework, rather than always harden, class difference. Under what conditions do encounters with poverty—be it proximate or distant poverty—entrench commonly held beliefs and assumptions about poor others? Under what conditions do encounters with poverty—be it a service learning trip to a distant continent or the view of a homeless body on the way to a sociology midterm—become what Lawson and Elwood (2014, 211) call "contact zones," which they define as "boundary-breaking, transformative moments" that "lead to new negotiations of identity, privilege, political responsibility and alliance"?

Finally, we argue in this book that the problem of global poverty, as constituted by poverty experts and global citizens, does not adequately capture the full extent of social inequality. Models of global citizenship pivot on the idea of the empowered global citizen who can, through sheer willpower and goodwill, end poverty. But it does not explain how poverty is produced and why it persists. Poverty experts are increasingly focused on economic and technological solutions to human suffering, but they struggle to understand why such solutions rarely make a dent in historically produced structures of deprivation and disempowerment. Most of all, they are unable to confront their own implication in the structures and processes that produce impoverishment. Thus philosopher Nancy Fraser (2010, 369) argues:

> To speak of "the poor" (global or otherwise) is, after all, to cast the people in question as passive victims instead of agents and potential political actors. It is also to see them in a free-standing, decontextualized way, in abstraction from the social relations and processes that have generated their poverty. To name their plight "poverty", finally, is to suggest that they simply, inexplicably lack the means of subsistence, whereas in fact they have been deprived of those means. For all these reasons, the expression "the global poor" fails to convey that the issue in question is one of injustice.

By eliding relations of impoverishment, dominant frames of global poverty suggest that the problem of poverty can be solved—by enthusiastic global citizens and well-meaning poverty experts. They, not the poor, become the agents of historical change. Thus, global poverty campaigns, intent on creating movements to end extreme poverty, forget that poor people's movements have been waging battle against impoverishment for a very long time. Here, it is instructive to return to Baudelaire's poetry. In the Global Poverty class, once our students have engaged with "The Eyes of the Poor," where the poor remain silent, staring at wealth but never speaking, demanding, or complaining, they are asked to read another poem by Baudelaire ([1869] 1970, 101–103), "Beat up the Poor." It describes a writer confronted by a beggar "with one of those unforgettable looks that would topple thrones." Gripped by the "Demon of action," the writer pounces on the beggar, beating him with a tree branch "with the obstinate energy of cooks trying to tenderize a beefsteak." His intent was this: "He alone is equal to another, if he proves it, and he alone is worthy of freedom, if he can conquer it." To the writer's delight, the beggar, "with a look of hatred," turns on him, beating him to a pulp with the same tree branch. Having verified the power of this "forceful medication," the writer acknowledges the beggar as his equal and asks him to do "the honor" of sharing his purse. Narrated from the vantage point of the writer who seeks to "restore" the "pride" and "life" of a beggar, the poem provokes questions that are of great relevance to today's poverty action: Who has the power to activate the agency of the poor? What are the grounds on which equality is established across the social classes? Who has the privilege to grant political recognition to the poor?

This moment of global poverty action has been made possible through the sustained struggle of poor people's movements. Emerging as protests against the ravages of structural adjustment and gaining momentum in the 1990s, a stunning proliferation of global collective action—from international peasant federations to antidebt movements—has challenged the status quo of economic globalization. Sociologist and activist Walden Bello (2007, 212) thus argues that such "people's resistance,"—"the decade-long people's counteroffensive"—has triggered a "crisis of the globalist project" and the "multilateral system of world economic governance." The organization founded by Bello, Focus on the Global South, is a good example of such global collective action. With offices in New Delhi, Manila, and Bangkok, Focus on the Global South (2015) seeks to "challenge neoliberalism, militarism and corporate-driven globalisation while strengthening just and equitable alternatives." It creates new imaginations and platforms of solidarity and alliance, envisioning the global South as "the great majority of humanity that is marginalized and dispossessed by globalization." On the one hand, it delegitimizes the institutions of economic globalization, such as the World Trade Organization, through protest and direct action. On the other hand, it produces forms of research, analysis, and knowledge that make possible alternative paradigms of globalization, economic prosperity, and democracy. Poor people's movements then are not simply a scramble for income and survival but also a profound struggle for equality. As American community organizer Saul Alinsky (1965, 41) once noted, poverty is not solely the "poverty of economy" but also the "poverty of power." Dominant frames of global poverty and dominant models of global citizenship do not address the poverty of power. However, the long history of poor people's movements must be read as the insistence for dignity, voice, and power. After all, the impoverished of the world are not mobilizing in mass action to demand malarial bed nets or TOMS shoes.

MAKING AND UNMAKING DEVELOPMENT

Two decades ago, the study of development was reshaped by a landmark text, *Encountering Development: The Making and Unmaking of the Third World,* written by anthropologist Arturo Escobar. Three arguments define the contributions the book has made to the field. First, Escobar presents the idea and practice of development as a Western project, which was imposed on the societies of Asia, Africa, and Latin America during the post–World War II period. Second, he (Escobar 1995, 7) notes that such a project relied on an "enframing" of the non-Western world as underdeveloped. This led to the emergence of the so-called Third World, defined by problems such as "poverty and backwardness" (Escobar 1995, 6). The project of development involved strategies for solving these problems, notably by interpreting the industrialized nations of North America and Europe as "indubitable models" of prosperity and modernity (Escobar 1995, vii). Third, Escobar (1995, 4) argues that the "dream" of development "turned into a nightmare." The "discourse and strategy of development produced its opposite: massive underdevelopment and impoverishment, untold exploitation and oppression."

This book, *Encountering Poverty,* is in conversation with Escobar's influential text. To encounter poverty, we argue, is not only to encounter "poor others" but also to be enlisted in the discourses and practices of development, those that seek to act upon poverty through specific techniques and interventions.

It is worth reflecting on the historical moment during which Escobar framed his arguments. *Encountering Development* ends with the call for a "postdevelopment era," the end to "forty years of incredibly irresponsible policies and programs" (Escobar 1995, 212). Indeed, as the book was being published, global social movements, especially those arrayed against the edifices of development, were gaining momentum. In 1994, activists marked the fiftieth anniversary of Bretton Woods, the conference that launched the post–World War II project of development, with the indictment: "Fifty Years is Enough!" Escobar's ideas, unfolding in a milieu shaped by these uprisings, generated a field of inquiry that may be understood as post-development thought, which is unrelentingly critical of the follies of development.

But Escobar's work, reinterpreted in this age of poverty, requires attention to the renewal and reinvention of development. Shaped by the legacies of post-development thought, we view our work as initiating a related field of inquiry, what we have dubbed critical poverty studies. Our concern is with how poverty has (re)emerged as a visible social problem on a global scale, how various types of expertise are being marshaled to diagnose and solve the problem of poverty, and how poverty action has become a place of encounters with "poor others" and thus of the negotiation of the boundaries of social class. Thus, we understand development to be a terrain of politics rather than a monolithic apparatus of dominance. In particular, we are interested in uncovering the aspirations that are mobilized and betrayed in poverty action and in the broader discourses and practices of development. These aspirations include those of what historian Vijay Prashad (2012) has described as the "poorer nations." Whereas Escobar was writing about development in the aftermath of structural adjustment, at a historical moment shaped by the rebellions against austerity, we write about poverty in a rearranged world, one in which the poorer nations are ascendant economies. As Escobar was able to analyze development as a project through which the West governed the Rest, today, development must also be understood as the project of postcolonial self-government (Roy 2014). Our use of the term "self-government" does not imply autonomy or sovereignty but rather a multipolar world order with new formations of economic hegemony and new alliances of power. In a 1989 speech at the World Bank, Manmohan Singh, who was then secretary general of the South Commission and would later become prime minister of India, declared that "new locomotive forces have to be found within the South itself" (Prashad 2012, 143). As a field of inquiry, critical poverty studies, shaped by post-development thought and yet departing from it, seeks to understand the peculiar problem of global poverty in this rearranged world.

A Rearranged World

Development studies scholar Gillian Hart (2001, 650) draws a distinction between development as a project and development as a process. The former, which she titles "big D Development," takes shape in the Bretton

Woods regime, "in the context of decolonization and the Cold War." Of course, its key impulses—such as techno-scientific improvement—have a much longer history, with important manifestations in nineteenth century colonialism. Hart calls the second type of development, "little d development," describing it as the "multiple, non-linear, interconnected *trajectories*" of the "development of capitalism." The problem of global poverty implicates both types of development. Situated in the interstices of the sprawling project of Development, global citizens and poverty experts grapple with the thorny question of whether the "end of poverty"—economist Jeffrey Sachs's (2005) influential phrase—is possible within the ongoing development of capitalism. We return to this profound dilemma in the next chapter of this book. Here, we situate global poverty in the context of a rearranged world and its renewed project of Development.

The start of the twenty-first century has been marked by a new world order of development and underdevelopment. On the one hand, the economies of the North Atlantic are in turmoil. From the Great Recession in the United States to what has been dubbed the existential crisis of the Eurozone, hitherto prosperous liberal democracies are finding themselves on shaky ground. In sharp contrast, in the economic powerhouses of the global South—for example, in India and China—new hegemonic models of capital accumulation are being put into place. And there is fast and furious experimentation with welfare programs and human development, be it the building of the world's largest development NGO in Bangladesh, the institutionalization of "right to the city" policies in Brazil, or the roll-out of ambitious poverty alleviation programs—such as conditional cash transfers—in many countries of South America. If sociologist Loïc Wacquant (2009, xi) has billed "America as the laboratory of the neoliberal future," then the global South can be understood as the laboratory of new experiments with development. For over a half-century, the Bretton Woods regime dominated discourses and practices of development. As expressed in the landmark speech of U.S. president Harry Truman in 1949, the Bretton Woods system was intended to make the "benefits of . . . scientific advances and industrial progress"—of the West—"available for the improvement and growth of underdeveloped areas" (Escobar 1995, 4). But today, a new architecture of economic and political power is reshaping development. Once dominant forces in development, institutions such as the World Bank and the International Monetary Fund (IMF), are now being matched by new development banks and monetary funds, such as the Bank of the South, for example. As the BRICS nations (Brazil, Russia, India, China, and South Africa) launch their own development bank, China emerges as the most important trading partner for Latin American and African countries, and the petro-wealth of countries such as Venezuela enables South-South flows of aid, those "indubitable models" (Escobar 1995, viii) of prosperity and modernity derived from the industrialized nations of North America and Europe are being refashioned or even discarded.

A key feature of this rearranged world is what economists Ravi Kanbur and Andy Sumner (2012, 687) have dubbed "the new geography of global poverty." Once concentrated in the world's poorest countries, the global poor now reside in middle-income countries, many of which are "stable" and "non-fragile" states, such as India, for example. These countries have "graduated" from low-income status to middle-income status, but such national prosperity has not made a significant dent in the persistent poverty that exists within their borders. Sumner (2013, 366) thus suggests that the question of global poverty must be reframed as a "matter of national distribution and domestic political economy."

The re-centering of development in the global South requires, as geographers Giles Mohan and Marcus Power (2009) argue, a "decentering" of the North in the study of development. It also requires, as Sumner (2013) notes, a rethinking of the conventional metrics through which the Bretton Woods regime has been understood, such as the flows of foreign aid, for example. Thus, in a recent report, the Organisation for Economic Co-Operation and Development (2014, 4), a multilateral forum, concludes that the "development finance landscape has changed dramatically in the last ten years." Foreign aid itself has become more diversified, with development assistance to countries in the global South flowing not only from the group of rich countries known as the DAC (the Development Assistance Committee of the OECD) but also from non-DAC countries. Other sources of development finance include private philanthropy and special purpose funds, such as climate funds. But equally significant is the dramatic increase in private capital flows, notably foreign direct investment and remittances, both from global North to global South and within the global South. In short, this is a rearranged world with a global institutional architecture that is markedly different than that of the Bretton Woods era.

It is tempting to interpret this new global architecture of development as a rupture with the discourses and practices of power analyzed by Escobar. Indeed, sociologist Jan Nederveen Pieterse (2011, 22) argues the "East-South turn" ends two hundred years of globalization dominated by "North-South relations." He finds that such a turn "holds significant emancipatory potential." We see this rearranged world and its new land-scapes of development finance as a terrain of contestation, one in which struggles over the meaning of poverty and the scope of poverty action are ongoing. We take seriously a note by sociologist Michael Goldman (2005, 37) in his ethnographic analysis of the World Bank, in which he contends that "development's 'failures'" generate "a creative effervescence," includ-ing new ideas and practices and new actors and networks. The age of pov-erty, with its millennial foot soldiers, is possibly such an effervescence.

There is also one more important point to make about global poverty in a rearranged world. In 1944, the year of the Bretton Woods conference, then U.S. president Franklin D. Roosevelt (1944), architect of the New Deal, laid out a Second Bill of Rights. He argued that the "inalienable political rights" that had undergirded the formation of the American republic were "inadequate" to tackle impoverishment. "True individual freedom," he noted, "cannot exist without economic security and inde-pendence." The Second Bill of Rights is an extraordinary vision, outlining rights that have still not been achieved in any part of the world, such as the "right to a useful and remunerative job," the "right of every family to a decent home," and the "right to a good education."

Inspired and mobilized by the Millennium Development Goals, the students in the Global Poverty and Practice Minor are profoundly moved by the Second Bill of Rights. They come to understand that it is not only a statement of hope but also a disclosure of the stark inequalities that haunt the "American standard of living." That standard of living was the aspira-tion that animated the Bretton Woods order. Yet Roosevelt (1944) trou-bles that aspiration: "We cannot be content, no matter how high that gen-eral standard of living may be, if some fraction of our people . . . is ill-fed, ill-clothed, ill-housed, and insecure. . . . America's own rightful place in the world depends in large part upon how fully these and similar rights have been carried into practice for all our citizens."

In a rearranged world, Roosevelt's critique of American prosperity and democracy is once again relevant. As the meticulous research of economists Thomas Piketty and Emmanuel Saez (2003) has demonstrated, income inequality in the United States is at a historic high, surpassing even the levels of inequality that preceded the Great Depression. Once understood as a condition imposed upon, and suffered by, the distant global South, austerity is now the context for the making of lives and livelihoods in the North Atlantic. If the 1980s was billed as the lost development decade in Africa and Latin America because of structural adjustment, then the Bush era of neoliberal redistribution can be billed as the lost decade for the American middle class (Pew Research Center 2012). To understand how such inequality was produced, it is necessary, as Saez (2013, 5) argues, to study the "retreat of institutions developed during the New Deal and World War II." At the margins of dominant models of global citizenship, a new generation of social activism is seeking to combat such retreat, tackling labor, income, and taxation policies. Amidst the college students and young professionals who flock to the Global Citizen Festival and sign up for overseas voluntourism are those that enlist in different types of movements, such as the battle to increase the minimum wage in various American cities, for example. Traces of the Second Bill of Rights are evident in their work.

Aspiration (or a Story of Three Millennials)

Each year, we have the opportunity to serve on the jury for a prize that supports research, creative work, and public service by undergraduate students to advance social justice. Millennials submit applications brimming with hope. There are projects to establish women's poetry collectives in Chiapas, Mexico, that will narrate and dismantle the hegemonies of patriarchy, nationalism, and neoliberalism. There is work to be done participating in the extraordinary civil rights struggles and supporting the dreams of undocumented American youth. There are efforts to combat financial predation and create financial protection for the poor in Bolivia. But in the age of poverty, millennials are enlisted not only in the unfinished work of freedom movements and civil rights organizing but also in the project of what anthropologist and sociologist Didier Fassin calls "humanitarian reason." Fassin (2011, xii) reminds us that in an unbearably unequal world, "humanitarianism elicits the fantasy of a global moral community" and often "fugaciously and illusorily bridges the contradictions of our world." Here are three glimpses of such humanitarian reason.

Carmen wants to return to Kenya to build solar ovens for communities of poor women living with HIV. She sees herself as an environmental educator committed to advancing "sustainability"—that ubiquitous shorthand that she uses in her application to place herself in a moral world. When asked why she wants to serve poor women in a village in Kenya, the vague phrase "cultural understanding" is her predictable response. But there is more. Carmen tears up and tells the jury that she wants to return to serve because it is only in that Kenyan village, surrounded by young children who make her feel welcome, that she has "felt human." For Carmen, who is a child of American prosperity and suburban alienation, this encounter with poverty is in fact a negotiation of her own humanity.

Rachel bursts into the room for her interview. A former White House intern with a resume filled with awards and accolades, she is confident and certain. She presents herself as a leader and entrepreneur who can teach poor youth in the battered neighborhoods of Richmond, California, that they too can be leaders and entrepreneurs, just like her. There is a catch though: the purpose of her project is for these youth to stay in their communities to ensure economic development for the troubled city. Rachel never mentions the towering Chevron oil refinery that sits atop the hills of Richmond. It is in the shadow of such power and exploitation that the aspiration to produce youth entrepreneurs must unfold.

Shalini is preparing to apply to medical school. A student with an impeccable GPA, she presents her engagement with poverty action as an experience that will make her a better doctor. She also candidly admits that without such humanitarian experience she will not be competitive for the top-ranked medical schools in North America. The budget accompanying her proposal includes a hefty fee to be paid to a third-party organization that will place her in an unpaid internship with a nonprofit health provider serving the poor in the remote rural regions of India, a common transaction in what must be understood as the vast industry of poverty action. Shalini is proud that, during this internship, she will be making medical diagnoses, prescribing medication, and even stepping in to do "minor surgeries" for the unserved. The image of premedical American students performing medicine on the bodies of the global poor, a transaction of benevolence mediated by the commodified transactions of the poverty action industry, is a chilling one. The room falls silent. We have reached the limits of humanitarian reason.

To understand the age of poverty, it is necessary to take serious account of the aspirations of millennials such as Carmen, Rachel, and Shalini. These aspirations are produced and deployed through the thoroughly commodified, and even industrialized, formats of service learning, short-term humanitarian missions, and voluntourism. Their stories indicate the ways in which entire professions—from medicine to engineering—are being reoriented to marry technical expertise with humanitarian reason. And as a result of this, millennials are positioned to exercise what social theorist Nikolas Rose (2000, 1399) terms "ethopower." Rose (2000, 1398–1399) argues that an era of "ethopolitics" is in the making, one in which human problems are "increasingly made intelligible as ethical problems," and where acting on such problems requires both "responsible self-government" and "the management of one's obligations to others."

It is important to note that such transactions of humanitarian reason are not limited to encounters between the West and the Rest. In an analysis of church trips taken by South Korean missionaries to East Africa, geographer Judy Han (2015) uncovers the imagination of development at work. She notes that South Korea, whose modern history presents a triumphant story of the defeat of poverty through Christianity, hardship, and compassion, is scripted as the developmentalist future of Africa. Such evangelical engagements with communities in underdeveloped regions of the world are a vital accompaniment of South Korea's ascension from being a country that was a receiver of foreign aid to becoming one that can afford to be a rich donor. It was the first formerly aid-receiving nation to become a member of the DAC. The Korean missionary project of upliftment in Africa is a consolidation of this heroic teleology of progress.

To understand the aspirations of millennials, it is necessary to consider the historical conjuncture that is the age of poverty. Such a conjuncture is marked by a rearranged world, one in which South Korea becomes an influential evangelist of development, for example. It is also marked by a new generation of global protest—in Cairo's Tahrir Square, in New York City's Zuccotti Park, in Istanbul's Gezi Park, in Madrid's Puerta del Sol Square, in Ferguson, Missouri, and in Baltimore, Maryland. Not necessarily poor people's movements, these are mobilizations that challenge the stark social, economic, and political inequalities of our times. Sociologist Manuel Castells (2012) has therefore described them as "networks of outrage and hope." From the Occupy movement in North America to the Indignado movement in Spain, these uprisings, he argues, seek to enact a deep "cultural transformation" of modern life. He notes that many of these movements have rejected the path of programmatic demands and instead advanced a critique of "a productivist vision of social action" (Castells 2012, 143). What Castells describes, perhaps with undue optimism, is what the Community Economies project, inspired by feminist geographers J. K. Gibson-Graham, has foregrounded as diverse forms of economic life that demonstrate that the economy can be a space of ethical action, an alternative to the capitalist economy (Gibson-Graham, Cameron, and Healy 2013). Active participants in the peer-to-peer economic transactions that have come to be dubbed the "sharing economy," our students are intrigued by such provocations. Can community economies be something more radical than Uber and Airbnb? In this book, we read global citizens and their poverty action as uncomfortably positioned in the contradictory spaces of sharing economies and community economies—the former an expression of global capitalism and its relentless search for new commodities, and the latter an instance of the effort to create alternative economic practices based on what Polanyi ([1944] 2001) once described as "reciprocity and redistribution."

Here, it is worth returning once again to the question of historical conjuncture. In 2011, *Time* magazine named Mark Zuckerberg, cofounder and CEO of Facebook, its 2010 Person of the Year. Zuckerberg was recognized for "connecting more than half a billion people and mapping the social relations among them, for creating a new system of exchanging information, and for changing how we live our lives" (Grossman 2010). Indeed, Facebook is the most obvious symbol of the era of digital democracy and its paradoxes, on the one hand enabling connectivity and on the other hand enabling enclosed identities as well as the enclosure of the digital commons. In 2012, *Time* named a quite different 2011 Person of the Year: "The Protester." They dubbed the protestor the "maker of history," noting that "massive and effective street protest . . . was the defining trope of our times" (Andersen 2011).

In this book, we read college students and young professionals immersed in poverty action—such as Carmen, Rachel, Shalini—as uncomfortably positioned in the contradictory global spaces of Facebook and street protest. We read them as negotiating the complex question of ethical action amidst global capitalism and its new formats of network economies. Such negotiation enmeshes them in humanitarian reason and poverty action. But at moments of rupture—those "contact zones" described by Lawson and Elwood (2014)—they come face to face with their own implication in relations of wealth and poverty, privilege and inequality. Instead of asking, "How do I help the poor?" they have to ask, "How is poverty produced, and what is my role in this process?" Instead of claiming the status of global citizen and asking, "How do I change the world?" they have to ask, "What is my role in the global economy and its inequalities?" The responses to such questions are varied. In some cases, they take the form of mending the new economy and softening its predatory impulses. In other cases, they take the form of outrage and protest against the long histories of exploitation and dispossession. Our work is an effort to honor the variety of responses and to use each as an occasion to think and act against inequality.

Expertise and Politics

In 1968, Robert McNamara became president of the World Bank. A key architect of the U.S. war in Vietnam, he assumed this role in tumultuous times. While the Lyndon Johnson presidency waged a domestic war on poverty, and the protracted civil rights movement was finally transforming the laws of the land, bitter protest swept through American cities against the bloodshed in Vietnam. But, at the World Bank, McNamara would define a new agenda for himself and for the Bretton Woods regime: poverty alleviation. In a landmark speech delivered to the World Bank's Board of Governors in Nairobi in 1973, McNamara argued that the institution had to tackle the problem of "absolute poverty," which afflicted "some 40% of the peoples of developing countries." Framing the matter as a moral issue, he asked: "Are not we who tolerate such poverty, when it is within our power to reduce the number afflicted by it, failing to fulfill the fundamental obligations accepted by civilized men since the beginning of time?" (Thurow and Kilman 2014, 30).

The McNamara World Bank represented a paradigm shift in development. Measures of economic growth, popular in the modernization frameworks of the first few decades of the existence of the World Bank, came to be replaced by a new emphasis on human development. As McNamara made poverty alleviation the responsibility of the World Bank—and, by extension, of rich, industrialized countries—so the relationship between poverty and economic growth had to be tackled, as was argued for in the unusual 1974 report *Redistribution with Growth*. In this way, as international relations scholar Martha Finnemore (1997, 204) notes, "poverty became a development 'problem.'" At the same time, the frame of global poverty transformed the project of development: "Before 1968, being 'developed' meant having dams, bridges and a (relatively) high GNP per capita. After 1973, being developed also required the guarantee of a certain level of welfare to one's population" (Finnemore, 1997, 206).

Needless to say, the McNamara World Bank did not end poverty. Despite the talk of structural change, through land reforms, for example, the development strategies of the McNamara years were "relatively modest, eminently possibilist, [and] bedeviled by political constraints" (Ayres 1983, 89). However, the problem of global poverty inaugurated important changes at the World Bank. Under McNamara, this development bank also became a "knowledge bank," launching a grand "new development science" about poverty, which was to have worldwide purchase (Goldman 2005, 72, 77). The World Bank dramatically expanded its operations, establishing new divisions and moving more money, through loans and concessional finance, than ever before. Indeed, it was by institutionalizing the problem of global poverty that the World Bank ensured its central role in development.

The McNamara World Bank gave way to the structural adjustment policies of the 1980s. A new development orthodoxy, one concerned with liberalization and privatization, engulfed the world. Instead of poverty alleviation, the Bretton Woods regime came to be concerned with promoting the magic of markets, what World Bank vice president and Nobel Prize–winning economist Joseph Stiglitz (2002, 36) was to later condemn as "market fundamentalism." It is from amidst the ravages of global austerity in the 1990s that the problem of poverty returned to the agendas of the World Bank, which was at that time under the presidency of James Wolfensohn. With protesters beating at the bank's door, Wolfensohn (2005) "put the spotlight back on the institution's true purpose—fighting global poverty and helping the world's poor forge better lives." But of course the Wolfensohn World Bank did not end poverty either. This assessment of the McNamara World Bank also applies to the bank under Wolfensohn's tenure: "In neither a national nor international sense did it seek fundamentally to change the world in which the poor lived; it sought to improve the terms on which they related to it" (Ayres 1983, 89).

This brief glimpse of the encounter between the World Bank and the problem of global poverty provokes important questions about expertise and politics, and these are central to the task of critical poverty studies. Take, for example, the idea of a knowledge bank. Imagining the role of the World Bank in the new millennium, Joseph Stiglitz (1999, 588) argues that it must not only address "a scarcity of capital, but a disparity in knowledge." Knowledge, he notes, is "one of the central international public goods," and it is the "special responsibility of the World Bank" to "close the knowledge gap" (Stiglitz 1999, 590). In particular, under Wolfensohn, the World Bank came to produce and disseminate authoritative knowledge about poverty. Producing reports bearing titles such as *Voices of the Poor* and *Listening to the Poor*, it positioned itself as the world's most influential poverty expert.

But the idea of a knowledge bank sits uneasily alongside another mandate of the Wolfensohn era: the country ownership of development. Part of the broader impulse to address the "democratic deficit" of which the Bretton Woods institutions have repeatedly been accused, country ownership is meant to reposition developing countries as stakeholders—rather than recipients—of development. Thus, one of the key tools of poverty governance, Poverty Strategy Reduction Papers, which are documents required by both the IMF and the World Bank, are meant to be "country-driven"—in other words, they are intended to promote "national ownership of strategies through broad-based participation of civil society." This is of course a quite complex formulation of the ownership of development—by national governments as well as by civil society actors. Needless to say, these different forms of ownership do not always neatly align with each other. If the World Bank is indeed the keeper of development knowledge, then in what ways do national governments own their poverty reduction plans? And how do these plans manifest "broad-based support from the public"?

Such questions about the politics of knowledge raise a related question: Who is the client of poverty-oriented development? After all, it is governments, not the poor, who are the clients of the World Bank. In a fascinating account of a meeting at the World Bank, scholar Bruce Rich (2002, 52) describes a senior manager confronting Wolfensohn: "Either we treat our governments as clients and we behave like merchant banks, in which case we owe it—again, to ourselves, in the first place, and to our counterparts, second—to stop talking about the environment, about women in development, about poverty alleviation, and so on as priorities. . . . If the government is not our client, the client is the people of the countries we work with, and the governments are agencies, instruments with whom we work to meet our clients' needs." Rich notes that Wolfensohn had to acknowledge the "real" and "perhaps insurmountable" contradiction that this challenge poses. He responded in a manner that reveals the limits of pro-poor development spearheaded by a development bank located at the heart of power in Washington, DC: "I obviously have perceived the task of moving from investment banking to development bank in a too-simplistic fashion. . . . We have a legal client that is the government. . . . We're ultimately serving the people. Ultimately. But our instrument is to work with government. I judge our effectiveness by the smile on the child's face in the village. I would extend it to the mother." Such are the profound dilemmas of expertise as it encounters the problem of poverty.

In seeking to analyze the age of poverty, we are also concerned with the forms and styles of poverty expertise. Escobar (1995, 35) notes that the professionalization and institutionalization of development through the discovery of poverty in the Bretton Woods era pivoted on a "faith in science and technology, invigorated by the new sciences arising from the war effort." This meant that problems of development could be cast as scientific problems, which were amenable to diagnosis and solution through science. As Escobar shows, one type of science in particular led the diagnosis of poverty and its solutions: development economics. Today's age of poverty also produces and deploys various types of scientific knowledge and professional practice. From a remaking of development economics as "poor economics"—Abhijit Banerjee and Esther Duflo's (2011) pithy phrase—to the emergence of fields of inquiry such as "development engineering," the problem of poverty is once again being located in specific domains of scientific expertise. The fact that these are powerful and well-resourced academic and professional domains—such as engineering, economics, business administration, and medicine—is significant. No longer consigned to the realm of social work or anthropological investigation, poverty is being refashioned in engineering labs, through microeconomic field experiments, and in places like Wall Street. In this book, we argue that the present historical conjuncture involves not only the (re)discovery of poverty on a global scale but also a distinctive (re)problematization of poverty as a techno-scientific problem. As we have already demonstrated, millennials too are implicated in the production of these dominant frames of global poverty, combining a yearning for calculated impacts and replicable solutions with ethopower. They are not only global citizens; they are also poverty experts. They too participate in what anthropologist Tania Murray Li (2007, 7), in an influential formulation, calls "rendering technical," how social problems come to be made "non-political"—for example, in the case of poverty, by obscuring "the practices through which one social group impoverishes another."

Ananya Roy at TEDx Berkeley, May 12, 2013,
"Un(Knowing) Poverty"
www.youtube.com/watch?v=pKASroLDF0M

But can the problem of poverty, never fully contained within the technical bounds of scientific expertise, politicize and disrupt powerful domains of knowledge? This too is a key question that we take up in this book. Li, in *The Will to Improve: Governmentality, Development, and the Practice of Politics,* her well-known ethnography of development interventions in the highlands of Indonesia, positions development as the "will to improve." However, she notes that there are enduring contradictions that accompany this will: "The first is the contradiction between the promotion of capitalist processes and concern to improve the condition of the dispossessed. The second is the way that programs of improvement designed to reduce the distance between trustees and deficient subjects actually reinscribe the boundary that positions them on opposite sides of an unbridgeable divide" (Li 2007, 27). We find Li's analysis of the contradictions of development to be a useful guide for critical poverty studies. In the age of poverty, efforts to reconcile capitalism and poverty alleviation abound. Following Li (2007, 21), such reconciliation can be understood to be an "awkward embrace."

But we depart from Li on one significant matter of expertise and politics. Li (2007, 2) argues that the "positions of critic and programmer are properly distinct." She notes that programmers, those who are tasked with implementing development, "under pressure to program better . . . are not in a position to make programming itself an object of analysis." We suggest that the project of development must itself be understood as a terrain of politics and that is therefore necessary to consider the ambivalences through which those charged with programming negotiate power and knowledge. Li goes on to suggest that the "more incisive critiques of improvement are generated by people who directly experience the effects of programs launched in their name of their well-being." Indeed, poor people's movements have generated such incisive critiques. Yet we are reluctant to conclude such a firm separation between the trustees and recipients of development. Instead, we interpret the mediators and functionaries of development—from star economists to young volunteers—to be engaged in the battle of ideas. Instead of positioning critics as those situated outside the project of development, we seek to explore how those within the system can participate in such struggles. However, we do not we want to overlook the fact that, often, the poor themselves are programmers of development, especially at the interface between bureaucracies of poverty and poor people's movements.

With this in mind, the opening reading of our sequence of Global Poverty classes at the University of California, Berkeley, is an essay penned

by Subcomandante Marcos of the Zapatista movement, titled "Do Not Forget Ideas Are Also Weapons." We assign this text to suggest to our students that they can be what Marcos (2000) describes as "progressive intellectuals" who "persist in criticising immobility, permanence, hegemony and homogeneity." The task of such critical thinkers, Marcos notes, is to be "skeptically hopeful." In contrast to the distinction that Li draws between programmer and critic, we work with the figure of the "double agent" (Roy 2010). Folded into structures of power, the double agent is ineluctably an expert. But can the encounter with poverty transform the expert into activist, albeit intermittently and temporarily? Can the double agent be subversive *within* the apparatus of development? Can millennials politicize humanitarian reason by recognizing the limits of solidarity in a highly unequal world? Working from within the pedagogy of global poverty, we seek to foster critical thinking and skeptical hopefulness among the foot soldiers of the age of poverty. In doing so, we occupy a space between two extremes: on one side is the hubris of benevolence (young Americans believing that they can solve the problem of poverty during an alternative spring break or a summer volunteer experience; poverty experts believing that the application of the right amount of scientific knowledge will enable the end of poverty) and on the other is the paralysis of cynicism (the unrelenting rejection of development and the deep distrust of powerful institutions such that the only options for knowledge and action are disavowal and withdrawal). This space is an impossible one, rife with contradictions and dilemmas. But occupying it, we believe, is the task and practice of critical poverty studies.

ENCOUNTERING POVERTY

In this chapter, we outlined a conceptual and pedagogical framework for rethinking how poverty is imagined and acted upon as a global problem. To do so, we presented three meanings of "encountering poverty." First, we foregrounded how, in an age of digitally visible poverty, college students and young development and advocacy professionals create a sense of self through encounters with poverty, both spatially distant poverty and spatially proximate poverty. Second, we noted that, also at work, is a renewed encounter between powerful knowledge systems, such as engineering and economics, and the problem of poverty. This encounter is constitutive of what is increasingly understood as "the global university"—highly competitive research institutions with global reach. The aspirations of millennials as global citizens are embedded in, and transform, the global university.

Third, we situated such encounters with poverty in the historical context of development, which we understand to be both ideology and an active worldwide project. That project is increasingly shaped by what was once seen to be "the poorer nations."

It is from within these encounters that we interrogate poverty as the dominant analytic for making sense of social difference and turn to other frames of thinking and acting against inequality. In doing so, we are attentive to the deep contradictions that attend poverty knowledge and poverty action. Perhaps the most significant of these contradictions is that the quest to "end poverty" rarely confronts the systems of exploitation that produce poverty. Instead, it is assumed that the very relations of impoverishment—such as the market economy—can be repurposed to mitigate poverty. We take up this matter more fully in the next chapter, "Governing Poverty." But we want to emphasize that global citizens, while keen to become poverty experts and poverty actors, are not ignorant of these contradictions. Instead of seeing them as dupes of capitalism, we uncover their self-critiques, their uncomfortable but constant negotiation of power, and their struggle to make lasting change in an unequal world. It is in this way that encounters with poverty haunt the public sphere, becoming a site at which profound questions about capitalism and liberal democracy must be posed.

Therefore, we neither celebrate nor denigrate poverty action, whether it be a rock concert in Central Park or a minimum wage campaign. Instead, we highlight "differentiated modalities of enlistment," a phrase we borrow from geographer Matthew Sparke (personal communication). We recognize that some of these modalities work within the interstices of neoliberalization, such as the impulse to build the perfect medical school application, complete with humanitarian work. Others agitate against neoliberalization and work in solidarity with long-standing struggles against exploitation and oppression, as in the renewed impulse for civil rights action. But, ultimately, we are optimistic about the plurality of such modalities of enlistment and about a historical conjuncture at which, at least in the global North, middle-class privilege is increasingly revealed to be fragile. From homeownership to college education, what were once anchors of economic security and social status are now tied up in unsustainable debt. This is a propitious moment to rethink not only the familiar narratives of poverty but also those of progress and prosperity.

3 Governing Poverty

Ananya Roy

> Development is the management of a promise—and what if
> the promise does not deliver?
>
> Jan Nederveen Pieterse (2000, 176)

IN THE CLASSROOM

On a sweltering day in September 2013, in the midst of what in the strange lexicon of the Anglo-American world is called an Indian summer, seven hundred students crowded into Wheeler Auditorium at the University of California, Berkeley, for their afternoon Global Poverty class. Given the theme of the course, they did not voice any complaints about the crowded room or the lack of air conditioning. After all, there were more important issues to ponder—notably, which of the two famous interlocutors of the global poverty debates was actually correct: William Easterly or Jeffrey Sachs? If students had flocked to this class in the hope of finding a blueprint for alleviating poverty, then the sharply contrasting views of Easterly and Sachs on foreign aid and development made it evident that there was no consensus on such matters. As the New York showdown—after all, Easterly and Sachs are firmly embedded in two competing but equally wealthy private New York universities—was reenacted in an austere public university classroom, students expressed a range of responses, from anguish to cynicism. I share here some of their live posts to the #GlobalPOV Twitter feed to provide a glimpse of how they entered into, and also transformed, the terms of the Easterly-Sachs debate. Such engagements are instructive for an understanding of how poverty is framed as a global problem.

> *@LillygolSedagha* Jeffrey Sachs sounds like Atlas taking on the weight of global poverty on his shoulders. It is a coalition not a personal mission #GlobalPOV

> *@jenniferfei* Millennium villages make me uncomfortable . . . There is no "single story" when it comes to poverty, thus no "single solution" #GlobalPOV

> *@Sarasindija* "development" is problematic presupposing an underdeveloped, a world of subaltern people needing us to "empower" them. #GlobalPOV

> *@TheBrewedBaker* The distribution of aid, which we talked about on Tuesday, verifies Easterly's claims about GOVERNMENT being the problem. #GlobalPOV

> *@OhSoSmriti* Though foreign aid has helped some situations, there is certainly no denying the parallels between aid and modern-day colonialism #GlobalPOV

> *@thatgirlmystic* The aid industry is an absolute disaster. See: Haiti #GlobalPOV

> *@Wyaat_* But how can I sleep in my king sized bed at night knowing my $4 didn't save the life of a child! D: #GlobalPov #Iactuallysleepinatwin

The tweets indicate how these students express an immediate affinity with the ideas put forward by William Easterly. Inhabitants of a post-welfare world, they carry with them a deep distrust of the role of government, an attitude that they quite seamlessly reconcile with their lives as students in a public university. Shaped by humanitarian reason, they are at once fully implicated in the optimism of poverty action and sharply critical of the failures of foreign aid. Crowding into a class on global poverty, they associate development with institutions like the World Bank and USAID, which, for them, are tainted. Their own practices of encountering and alleviating poverty are, in their minds, a different genre of intervention— not the social engineering that Easterly disgraces as "planning" but rather the incremental, free-spirited problem solving that he advocates as "searching." The global Keynesianism so vigorously propounded by Jeffrey

Sachs makes them uneasy. Although they champion Sachs's call to "end poverty," they cannot share in his enthusiasm for a "big push" to assist countries to ascend the "ladder of development."

Over the years, my own teaching of the Global Poverty class has shifted. I find myself much more impatient with the halo of volunteerism that my students like to wear, which they embrace in opposition to what they perceive to be the "system," be it government or aid agencies. I find it paradoxical that they ignore how their middle-class lives are buttressed by numerous forms of government support—which I like to call welfare— while many of them are committed to the ideology that aid and welfare are bad for the poor. And so, as my students were tweeting their way through the Easterly-Sachs debate (their tweets made the #GlobalPOV hashtag trend for an afternoon), I was engaged in my own Twitter conversation with @JeffDSachs, reflecting on the pedagogy of global poverty, its limits, and its possibilities. Figure 3.1 gives an excerpt of that conversation.

Yet, on that Indian summer day, my students also recognized the limits of the contemporary debates about global poverty. With sarcasm, they foregrounded the long histories of colonialism and capitalism so often obscured in the Easterly-Sachs showdown. Fully implicated as a generation in the quest to solve the problem of poverty, they knew that neither Sachs's big push nor Easterly's "Searchers" could solve the historic inequalities produced by racial and colonial dispossession. Increasingly steeped in common sense about economic injustice, which has recently been brought to the fore by the Occupy movement, they expressed concern not about a "poverty trap" but rather about an "affluence trap." Unknowingly, they echoed the work of economist John Kenneth Galbraith (1958), who, over a half century ago, was writing about the dangers of America's "affluent society." Separated by several generations from the anticolonial struggles of the twentieth century, the students unknowingly echoed the language of decolonization. Frantz Fanon ([1961] 2007, 55), a philosopher and revolutionary, noted that "the basic confrontation which seemed to be colonialism versus anti-colonialism" was "already losing its importance." "What matters today, the issue which blocks the horizon," he argued, "is the need for a redistribution of wealth." The global citizens of 2013 were arguing that the basic confrontation was far from over and that

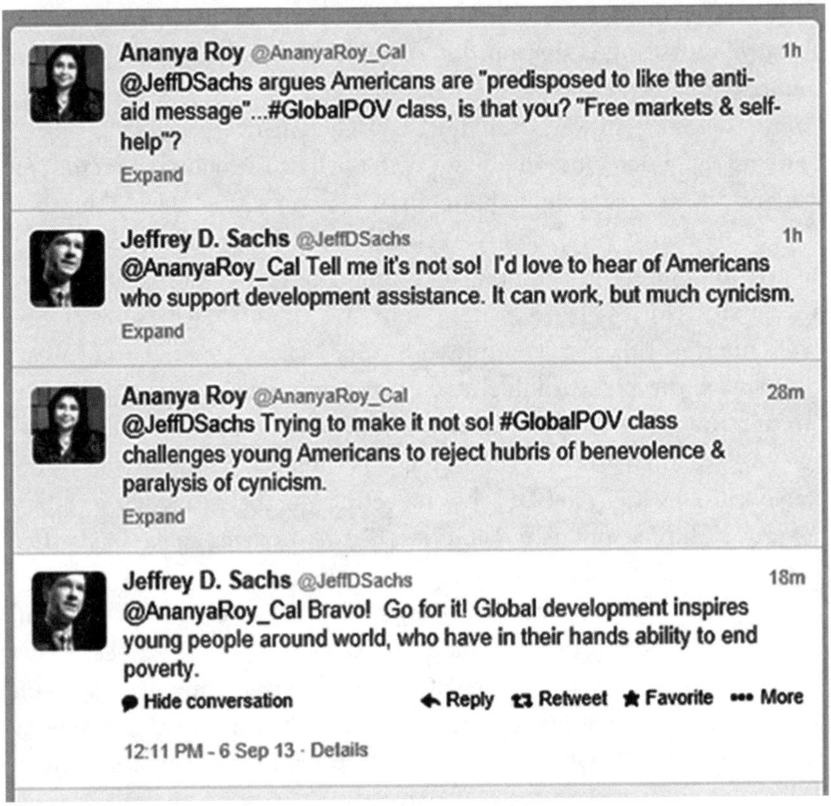

Figure 3.1. A Twitter exchange between Ananya Roy and Jeffrey Sachs, 2013.

the redistribution of wealth could not be separated from histories of exploitation and extraction. Here are some of those tweets:

@*SandraGuzmanGPP* #GlobalPOV Big Push v. Small Pushes. It took centuries for the North to impoverish the South such situation that can't be 'fixed" overnight.

@*takearidewithme* The West never had to climb a ladder. They stumbled onto the "roof", and created a ladder to make sure the Rest are always below. #GlobalPOV

@*amin_uzma* "Geographic disadvantage is a euphemism for colonialism." @AnanyaRoy_Cal #GlobalPOV

@DJaramillo13 Fighting poverty with capitalism. Riiiiight . . . #GlobalPOV

@LaakeaSky If the West were to assist in poverty alleviation it would be more an amends than an act of altruism. #GlobalPOV

@gborgej Is #globalpov the white man's burden or is it the white man in fact sitting on a poor man's back, choking him, and making him carry him?

@RaiseTheWageEB Berkeley is the most economically unequal city in the Bay Area. Poverty Trap & Affluence Trap right under our noses #GlobalPOV

THE PUZZLES OF POVERTY

A few years ago, as the World Bank was in the process of appointing a new president—an undertaking in which the U.S. government has always wielded disproportionate power—Jeffrey Sachs made the case for his candidacy. He promised to apply "science and knowledge" to the world's most urgent human development problems: "flooded villages, drought-ridden farms, desperate mothers hovering over comatose, malaria-infected children, and teenage girls unable to pay high school tuition" (Sachs 2012). Sachs's proposals speak to the immediate reality of global poverty, but they also hearken to a previous era, to the 1950s and 1960s, when development economists such as Walt Rostow formulated plans to modernize backward economies and U.S. presidents like Harry Truman boldly announced the deployment of American scientific advances that would mitigate the underdevelopment of the Third World. William Easterly (2012), who had already been dubbed "the man without a plan" by Nobel laureate Amartya Sen (2006), responded to Sachs's bid with a tongue-in-cheek essay expressing gratitude for his own "non-nomination for World Bank president." He wrote: "I would not lead the World Bank by assembling an expert task force of my fellow social scientists, natural scientists, and random unemployed politicians. I would not ask such a well-qualified expert task force to answer the question 'What must we do to end world poverty?'—especially if we forget to answer the question 'Who put us in charge?'"

Here, then, are two fundamentally different visions of development. One views development as a comprehensive plan through which scientific expertise, financed by foreign aid, can be used to solve poverty, an approach that Sachs terms "clinical economics." Take, for example, the Millennium Villages in Africa, where Sachs led the implementation of an integrated package of interventions targeting agricultural production, health, education, and infrastructure. The contrarians view this type of development as "a technocratic illusion," a form of authoritarianism that is "rule by experts." The other vision views poverty, in Easterly's words, not as the "shortage of expertise" but rather as "the shortage of rights." "Authoritarian development," a system in which "well-intentioned autocrats" are "advised by technical experts," only exacerbates this shortage by deepening the "unchecked power of the state against poor people without rights" (Easterly 2014: 6–7).

There is quite a bit at stake in the Easterly-Sachs debates, notably the relevance of foreign aid in the reduction of poverty. But there are also some puzzles that haunt both approaches to development, those that indicate that the man with a plan and the man without a plan might not be so far apart in their worldviews. One is the puzzle of markets, and the other is the puzzle of colonialism. The two are in fact part of the same puzzle, that of the relationship between capitalism and poverty. This, as we noted in the previous chapter, is the most significant contradiction that haunts the present age of poverty knowledge and action.

"The Wretched of the Earth"

During the last gasp of the unbearably long occupation of Algeria by France, Frantz Fanon ([1961] 2007) wrote a seminal analysis of the dehumanizing effects of colonialism, *The Wretched of the Earth*. Decades later, without reference to Fanon, Amartya Sen (2006) invokes the same turn of phrase when reviewing Easterly's arguments about development, noting that Easterly's work "is about the imprisonment of the world's poor in the trap of international aid, where 'planners' have incarcerated the wretched of the earth." Indeed, on most days, Easterly sounds like Fanon, or at least like critical development theorists who draw on the traditions of postcolonial thought established by philosophers such as Fanon. Easterly's phraseology—"rule by experts," "neotrusteeship," "the ideology of development"—is reminiscent of the influential critiques of development by anthropologists and political theorists such as James Ferguson, Arturo Escobar, Timothy

Mitchell, and Tania Murray Li. Such scholarship is keenly aware of the colonial roots of development thought and practice. In a similar vein, Easterly (2013, 44) argues that "development ideas took shape while racism and colonialism still reigned supreme." Discussing the effects of colonialism, including "failed states and bad governments," Easterly (2014, 272) sharply criticizes today's development efforts as "a new White Man's Burden to clean up the mess left behind by the Old White Man's burden."

Sachs is not silent on the question of colonialism either. In seeking to explain the "vast gulf" between rich countries and poor countries, he notes "the brutal exploitation of dominant colonial powers," even suggesting that such exploitation, dispossession, and "even slavery" were key ingredients of modern economic growth (Sachs 2005, 50, 39). But ultimately for Sachs, such colonial histories are not decisive. "The basic underlying forces that propelled the Industrial Revolution," he argues, "could be and were replicated elsewhere," through what he describes as a "cascade of technological change" (Sachs 2005, 39, 41). Alongside his descriptions of colonial violence, Sachs tells the story of the diffusion of prosperity through the "transmission of technologies and the ideas underlying them" (Sachs 2005, 41). He arrives at the following conclusion: "This is why we can envision a world in which everyone achieves prosperity" (Sachs 2005, 41).

But what then explains the wretched of today's earth? For Sachs, the causes lie in a series of "poverty traps," including, most notably, geographic disadvantage. Impoverished places, he suggests, "are shaped profoundly by their location, neighborhood, topography, and resource base" (Sachs 2005, 105). These factors, of course, can be overcome with the right package of interventions, as in the case of the Millennium Villages. "Poverty to Sachs," Easterly (2006a, 101) thus notes, "seems to be a technical problem that can be fixed with interventions from the natural sciences." By contrast, Easterly believes that poverty is decidedly not a technical problem. Nor is development a technical solution. Colonialism matters to Easterly because it is the precedent to today's authoritarian development, thus evoking that central (political, not technical) question: "Who put us in charge?"

But the puzzle of colonialism also speaks to a different question: What is the relationship between wealth and poverty? This is the question our students were wrestling with as they sought to interpret the Easterly-Sachs debate, the question that reveals that colonialism is not just an era that has ended—as Sachs would have us believe—but rather a living history that is present in various relations of exploitation and dispossession. Key to colonialism is what Fanon ([1961] 2007, 3) identifies as "geographic configuration," a violent ordering of space and society. The colonized world is thus, as Fanon eloquently describes it ([1961] 2007, 5), "a famished sector, hungry for bread, meat, shoes, coal and light . . . a sector that crouches and cowers, a sector on its knees." This analysis of the colonized world is not just of elsewhere, it is also of "here," of the "famished sector" at the heart of the rich countries who are at the top of the ladder of development. From Jim Crow segregation to today's militarized homeland borders, racial segregation and domination, expressed in geographical separation, is constitutive of modern prosperity. Impoverished places do not suffer from the natural causes of geographic disadvantage; rather, these places are produced through relations of racialized control and exclusion, which in turn produce persistent poverty.

We have reached, then, the limits of contemporary frames of global poverty. Even Easterly (2006b, 278) is ultimately ambivalent about the nature of colonialism, attributing its effects to "incompetence" rather than "avarice." It is an ambivalence that obscures the relationship between wealth and poverty, that paradoxically reinforces a fundamental certainty about modern economic growth and its diffusion of prosperity. Such certainty is shaken up when we try to explain the persistence of poverty— brutal and obscene poverty—in the rich countries. In his remarkable sociological treatise, *The Souls of Black Folk,* published in 1903, W. E. B. Du Bois ([1903] 1994: 5)wrote of life in America: "To be a poor man is hard, but to be a poor race in a land of dollars is the very bottom of hardships." Such poverty is not the unfortunate supplement to wealth; rather, it is the very basis of the land of dollars. Thus, in his much-acclaimed work, *Capital in the Twenty-First Century,* Thomas Piketty (2014, 161) draws attention to the importance of slavery in U.S. fortunes, noting that in the antebellum South, "slave capital largely supplanted and surpassed landed capital." It was a world in which, quite literally, "one half of the population owned the other half." He concludes his analysis with the poignant line, "This no doubt accounts for the many aspects of the development—or rather nondevelopment—of the US welfare state" (Piketty 2014, 162). It is a point to which I will return later in this chapter.

"Malaria Is Not a Market . . . It's a Pandemic Disease"

In her important exposition of neoliberalism, Naomi Klein (2010, 176) describes the exploits of Jeffrey Sachs as those of an "economic shock doctor" implementing "shock therapy," a draconian package of free market economic reforms, in countries such as Bolivia, Poland, and Russia in the 1980s. This kind of so-called shock therapy was a key part of what Joseph Stiglitz (2002, 36) describes as the ideology of "market fundamentalism," an ideology that, he argues, pervaded the institutions that govern globalization (the IMF, the World Bank, and the WTO) and that set into motion a fury of discontents around the world.

But more recently, Sachs has had a change of heart. Instead of the dramatic imposition of liberalization and privatization, he is now intent on ending extreme poverty through economic development. Instead of free market reforms, he is the most prominent voice calling for the implementation of the UN's Millennium Development Goals. Instead of austerity, he boldly calls for a global Keynesianism funded by dramatic increases in foreign aid from rich countries to poor countries. Although Sachs presents his current role as a "clinical economist" as an extension of his earlier work, surely the economic and social disasters wrought by economic shock therapy, especially in Russia, shaped his conversion to humanitarian reason. Most significantly, Sachs now argues that urgent human problems such as poverty, disease, and hunger cannot be solved through markets. "Malaria," he declares, "is not a market. . . . It is a pandemic disease and a killer" (Munk 2013, 99). But perhaps what has not changed is his faith in the power of technocracy. "For Sachs," Klein (2010, 252) writes of the economist's years as a shock doctor, "the making of history is a purely elite affair, a matter of getting the right technocrats settled on the right policies." So is it today with his global campaigns against poverty.

In a scathing critique, Easterly (2006b, 14) dismisses Sachs's ideas as simply the latest schemes in a long string of failed "Big Western Plans" seeking to end poverty. As an alternative to such "utopian social engineering," Easterly draws our attention to two processes. The first is "homegrown development," in which sovereign nation-states pursue their own strategies of economic growth. This, he notes, is the case of economic powerhouses such as India and China. The second is "piecemeal efforts," and it lies at the heart of Easterly's alternative vision of development. Described variously as "searching" or "free development," this is a mode of problem solving that Easterly views as incremental and autonomous, undertaken by free individuals with political and economic rights. He insists that development must depart from the "tyranny of experts," as the world's poor are "their own best searchers" (Easterly 2006b, 27). There is, of course, a quite striking contradiction between these two pieces of Easterly's vision. Homegrown development sits uneasily alongside free development, especially in instances of powerful developmental states implementing strategies of economic prosperity, often through heavy-handed means. Easterly ignores this contradiction, as he does the warnings Sachs, Stiglitz, and others make about market failure. Instead, he celebrates the market as the source of innovation: "Individualism and decentralized markets were good enough to give rise to penicillin, air conditioning, high-yield corn, and the automobile—not to mention better living standards, lower mortality, and the iPod" (Easterly 2007). For Easterly (2006b), then, markets are the ideal form of problem solving, and this leads him to his famous diagnosis of poverty: "The rich have markets, the poor have bureaucrats."

It is tempting to reduce the Easterly-Sachs debate to a discussion of markets versus governments. Indeed, our students often think that they have to pick sides: destructive markets or destructive governments? But the debate actually reveals important insights into how frames of global poverty turn on particular conceptualizations of markets. Easterly relies, for example, on the idea of free markets. He believes that markets "everywhere emerge in an unplanned, spontaneous way" (Easterly 2006b, 61, 69), which leads him to conclude that "free markets work, but free market reforms don't."

It is instructive to contrast this notion of the spontaneous order of markets with a different economic history. Take, for example, *The Great Transformation*, political economist Karl Polanyi's ([1944] 2001) masterful account of the emergence of the market economy in the West. In this book, Polanyi shows how the "self-adjusting market" is a "stark utopia." It comes into existence not as a spontaneous order but rather through the violent transformation of labor, nature, and human exchange into commodities. But Polanyi ([1944] 2001, 3) argues that such an arrangement, which is based solely on self-interest, verges on the annihilation of the "human and natural substance of society." In response, a new order is created, often spontaneously, embedding the economy in social life and creating a "society with markets" rather than "market societies."

In his foreword to the 2001 edition of *The Great Transformation*, Joseph Stiglitz (Polanyi [1944] 2001, vii) applies Polanyi's ideas to the contemporary problem of poverty: "Polanyi's analysis makes it clear that the popular doctrines of trickle-down economics—that all, including the poor, benefit from growth—have little historical support." But what is equally significant is Polanyi's debunking of the very idea of free (i.e., self-adjusting) markets and their spontaneous order. The market economy, he repeatedly insists, is not natural but rather a system of "extreme artificiality," created not as a spontaneous, grassroots order—as Easterly would have us believe—but rather through "interventionism," specifically "deliberate state action" (Polanyi [1944] 2001, 77, 146–7). Planning, or social protection, he notes, is what emerged spontaneously as an effort to curb the devastating effects of the free market. In a stunning line, Polanyi ([1944] 2001, 147) concludes: "Laissez-faire was planned; planning was not." His argument is a sharp and significant departure from that of his peer, the economist Friedrich von Hayek, whose book *The Road to Serfdom*, which was also published in 1944, made the case for the virtues of the free market and the dangers of centralized planning.

Once again, we have reached the limits of contemporary frames of global poverty. Easterly and Sachs may indeed disagree vigorously on the question of market failures and market innovations, one relying on Hayek and the other on Keynes. But ultimately, they are united in what Sheppard (2011, 59) describes as "consensus on the question of development," or in other words, on the prospect of globalizing capitalism, whether in the form of free markets or adjusted through state interventions, to generate widespread prosperity. Ultimately, Sachs and Easterly are united in their view that global poverty is a problem to be solved. It is this problem-solving spirit that animates millennials as they puzzle over the methods and techniques of solutions. But what if we were to heed a different line of thought about development, such as that of Latin American economic and political theorists writing in the 1950s and 1960s about "the development of underdevelopment" (Frank 1966)? What if, instead of the ladder of development, we were to recognize that the prosperity of wealthy places often depends on the impoverishment of other places and peoples? And what if, following Polanyi, we were to realize that this is not the natural order of things but rather a system of extreme artificiality? These are the questions that are so often avoided in prevalent and popular frames of global poverty. Yet these are the very questions that must be tackled.

SOLVING PROBLEMS

For all their differences, Easterly and Sachs are united in the idea that economic growth—achieved through markets, trade, entrepreneurship, and innovation—will ultimately solve the problem of poverty. It is this impulse to frame poverty as a problem that can be solved and the firm faith in the spread of economic prosperity that are defining characteristics of the age of poverty. Throughout this book, we investigate this impulse and this faith more closely through key examples of poverty action. In doing so, we problematize the problem of poverty. Philosopher Michel Foucault describes problematization as the set of practices through which something comes to be constituted as an object of concern, reflection, or thought. Problematizing means analyzing how an "ensemble of difficulties" has several possible responses and noting that some responses emerge as dominant and prevalent (Rabinow 2004, 43). But it also means analyzing what Foucault calls the "space of knowledge." Who has the power to inhabit such a space and thus frame a problem? Foucault ([1969] 2002, 5) insists that we ask: "Who is speaking? . . . What is the status of the individuals who—alone—have the right, sanctioned by law or tradition . . . to proffer such a discourse?" Here are three problem spaces, each of which allows for a problematization of the problem of poverty.

Bottom-Billion Capitalism

In the age of poverty, there is a proliferation of intimate portals of action, each promising a solution to the problem of poverty. "Empower people around the world with a $25 loan," promises Kiva.org, an online platform that allows anyone with intent and means to efficiently and immediately make microfinance loans to the poor. Inspired by the slogan, "Improving lives with every purchase," a grocery store chain acclaimed for its organic and sustainable food has set up change boxes at their checkout counters, allowing customers to drop in a dollar to make a contribution toward fighting world hunger. When customers buy a pair of TOMS shoes, they know that a second pair will be donated to a child in need, a "one-for-one" reciprocity with a simple symmetry. Such forms of poverty action can be understood as ethical consumerism, a set of ideas and practices that seek to solve the problem of poverty through better choices made by consumers. Two elements are central to ethical consumerism. The first is the concept of the empowered citizen. Take, for example, (RED), a campaign that donates a portion of the profits from the sale of (RED)-branded products—be it a set of Beats headphones or an iPod—to the Global Fund to fight AIDS, Tuberculosis, and Malaria. The (RED) manifesto, available on the organization's website, declares: "We all have tremendous power. What we choose to do or even buy, can affect someone's life on the other side of the world." The second is the idea that ethical consumerism is a display. A dizzying array of choices for poverty action are presented to the empowered consumer, mimicking the overstocked shelves of the prosperous world and often taking on the form of striking visual spectacles of poverty and need. Take, for example, Heifer International, an organization that offers do-gooders a catalog of "life-changing gifts," such as a cow for a needy family, which its website describes as a "full package of training and assistance" that will give the "gift of women's empowerment." In the late nineteenth century, world exhibitions hosted in European cities such as London and Paris put on display the exotic wonders of the colonized world. What was at stake was not only the power to represent subordinated peoples and their histories through exhibits and images but something bolder: "to image the world as exhibition" (Mitchell 1991). Today, a similarly bold imperative is at work in the exhibition of poverty as a problem that can be solved through the rational choices of the ethical but prosperous consumer.

The #GlobalPOV Project, *Can We Shop to End Poverty?*
www.youtube.com/watch?v=mpuf-N66CGI

Ethical consumerism is the topic of one of our #GlobalPOV videos, *Can We Shop to End Poverty?* When we were preparing the storyboard for the video, we knew we wanted to feature some of the images of the global poor that were on display at the Berkeley location of a well-known national grocery retail chain. Everywhere in the store, shoppers were surrounded by photographs of smiling poor entrepreneurs, usually women, whose lives were supposedly being improved by their purchases. The store's expensive food was being made ethical through the magical promise that lives elsewhere were being transformed by microfinance, the preferred modality of poverty alleviation of the philanthropic foundation associated with the retail chain. With each donation, shoppers themselves became micro-philanthropists, empowering poor women they would never know or meet.

But our script for the video generated great anguish for the foundation. Their spokesperson refused to grant us permission to use their images or photograph within their stores unless we changed the script. In particular, the line, "Do the poor really smile this much?" rankled her. In an impassioned response, she argued that the poor women entrepreneurs featured in the foundation's publicity material and widely displayed at all the chain's grocery stores were smiling because they were proud of their microenterprises. The smile, she emphasized, is a statement of human dignity, and above all, it is a sign of a new type of economy, one based on a stakeholder business model in which the poor gain social benefit from global capitalism. "Why don't you pick on a store that does not care to help the communities from which it sources its products?" she asked.

I share this story because it encapsulates key elements of what I term "bottom-billion capitalism," a transformation of capitalism that integrates the world's poorest one billion people, not through well-worn formats of exploitation and dispossession but rather through new formats of inclusion. The term encompasses, for example, the idea of "conscious capitalism"—a commitment to achieving social impact while simultaneously reaping profits—which has been promoted by American businessman John Mackey (Mackey, Sisodia, and George 2013), and Bill Gates's (2008) vision of "creative capitalism," which involves overhauling capitalism so that it includes and assists the billions that, until now, have been excluded. Key to conscious or creative capitalism is the "heroic spirit"—

Mackey, Sisodia, and George's phrase—of markets, an idea that bears striking resemblance to Easterly's enthusiasm for the problem-solving capacity of decentralized markets. Perhaps the most influential exposition of this idea comes in the work of business school guru C. K. Prahalad (2004), who argues that it is possible to eradicate "poverty through profits." In his early work, Prahalad envisioned the world's poor as vast and new markets, a source of renewed profits for corporations. Most significantly, Prahalad argued that such an approach would break with paternalistic forms of aid to the poor. The cover of his book *The Fortune at the Bottom of the Pyramid* bears the phrase, "enabling dignity and choice through markets." However, in his later work, Prahalad more ambitiously argues that the bottom of the pyramid is a "giant laboratory" where the "next practices" of business models and strategies could be found. In short, multinational corporations could discover "new sources of value from the social practices of the poorest of the poor" (Elyachar 2012, 110). These efforts to create and promote bottom-of-the-pyramid (BoP) markets also turn on a specific conceptualization of poverty, that of the inherent entrepreneurialism of the poor.

A prominent example of bottom-billion capitalism is microfinance, the provision of financial services to the poor. Microfinance has become a poverty panacea. Billed as the democratization of capital, it seeks to remedy exclusionary systems of finance by extending credit to the poor. Targeting mainly women, it is seen to be an effective instrument of gender empowerment. But most significantly, microfinance is considered to be a potentially profit-making BoP market. Promoted aggressively by the World Bank and other development donors, commercial microfinance is thus concerned with the double bottom line of profit and poverty alleviation. Indeed, microfinance promoters have argued that only a profit-making industry with high financial returns can transform the lives of the bottom billion. Such is the optimism accompanying various microfinance launches on the stock market. For example, in 2010, SKS Microfinance Ltd., one of India's largest microfinance institutions, had an initial public offering of $347 million in stock. SKS's investors, including Silicon Valley venture capitalist and cofounder of Sun Microsystems, Vinod Khosla, reaped handsome profits in the millions of dollars. In keeping with the broader ethos of bottom-billion capitalism, Khosla argued that what was at stake was a profit-making, and therefore sustainable, approach to poverty alleviation: "There is not enough money to be given away in the world to make the poor well off" (Bajaj 2010).

But just a few months after the global headlines about the SKS IPO, microfinance was in the news again, but this time for quite different reasons. The reports now focused on a spate of suicides seemingly triggered by microfinance debt—labeled "India's microfinance suicide epidemic" (Biswas 2010)—as well as on a growing revolt by microfinance borrowers. Coming from the same villages of south India served by SKS Microfinance, these stories of microfinance were not accompanied by smiling poor women entrepreneurs. Instead, they were testimonials of despair and death. Suddenly, microfinance, the icon of bottom-billion capitalism, was being compared to the crisis of subprime loans that had rocked the housing market in the United States and triggered the Great Recession of 2007–2009.

The #GlobalPOV Project, *Who Profits from Poverty?*
www.youtube.com/watch?v=0deJfPUj1f8

In my research, I argue that it is instructive to consider the analogy between microfinance and subprime lending (Roy 2010). The concept of subprime raises the question of why certain social groups can only access credit and other financial services on terms that are less advantageous than those offered to "prime" borrowers. In the U.S. context, such designation of risk has been a deeply racialized phenomenon, a continuation of older practices of racial segregation, such as redlining. Geographer Elvin Wyly and his colleagues (2008) thus note that "exclusionary denial and inclusionary segmentation into subprime credit are two sides of the same coin." In the case of microfinance, we have to ask what financial inclusion means when poor women are expected to pay interest rates of nearly 100 percent for commercial microfinance loans. This may be the creativity of capitalism, but it is also akin to what a *Business Week* report calls America's "poverty business," the predatory practices of "ambitious corporations" that see profits in "thin wallets" (Grow and Epstein 2007). Key to the poverty business is "opportunity pricing," the setting of prices not on the basis of the value of the commodity or service being sold but rather on an assessment of how much payment can be extracted from the impoverished consumer. So it is with commercial microfinance. The famous mantra, "the poor always pay back," is less a statement about the morality of the poor or a valuation of the microenterprises of the poor and more an indication of the capacity of microfinance institutions to aggressively pursue debt collection—that is to say, the poor can always be *made* to pay back. Equally key to the poverty business is that profits are privatized while losses are socialized. The financial benefits of opportunity pricing or a microfinance IPO are reaped by a handful of corporations and billionaire investors and, in the best cases, also by their stockholders. But the devastations of such "deregulated market innovation" are borne not only by those who suffer "inclusionary discrimination"—Wyly et al.'s (2008) poignant phrases—but also, more broadly, by society, through the sheer social, economic, and political impact of such systems of speculation and opportunism. The pro-poor market, just like the self-adjusting market, may very well be a stark utopia. We may have reached the limits of bottom-billion capitalism.

But what if we were to trace a different history of microfinance? After all, microfinance is one of those rare development ideas that originated in the global South and was then taken up by powerful development institutions in the global North. Pioneered in Bangladesh in the late 1970s by organizations such as the Grameen Bank and BRAC, microfinance did not diffuse from the West to the Rest. Instead, it emerged in the crucible of an independence movement and its optimistic aftermath of nation-building. Microfinance was the energetic expression of a homegrown civil society, entangled from the very start—especially in organizations such as BRAC—with the political imperative to organize the rural landless in the context of semifeudal agrarian inequality. Interestingly, while the concept of microfinance diffused globally, quickly becoming a rather simplistic formula of bottom-billion capitalism, in Bangladesh it remained embedded in ambitious experiments with human development and social protection. Fazle Abed, the founder of BRAC, the Bangladesh-based international NGO, calls this approach "microfinance plus." Indeed, as my research shows, credit services are only a small part of the Bangladesh model of microfinance (Roy 2010). Much more vital are savings programs, asset-building and safety net strategies, legal aid and insurance assistance, social enterprises, and a massive human development infrastructure ranging from primary schools to health clinics. Behind the public transcript of entrepreneurial poor women magically crafting microenterprises from tiny loans—a narrative that still defines the work of the world's most famous microfinance institution, the Grameen Bank—lies this hidden transcript. Most boldly, organizations such as BRAC have decisively intervened in the key sectors of the economy that impact the lives and livelihoods of the poor, such as dairy production, the poultry industry, aquaculture, and farming. Creating new distribution channels and value chains, these interventions do not rely on the invisible hand of the market to deliver innovations to the poor but instead leverage the formidable power of a vast nonprofit organization, in this case BRAC, to ensure a more fair and equitable economy. There is nothing bashful about this kind of Big Plan, implemented at massive scale by centralized and bureaucratic organizations. Anything less, Abed has said, will be "tinkering around on the periphery" of social change (Armstrong 2008).

What we have in Bangladesh, then, is a model of human development that is neither the Rostowian "big push" advocated by Sachs nor the home-grown market-led innovations advocated by Easterly. Despite being saddled with political instability and sputtering economic growth, Bangladesh continues to far outpace its neighbor India on key human development indicators, such as primary education and basic health, a phenomenon that has been dubbed the "Bangladesh paradox." In the process, a new discourse of poverty is generated. Although this discourse still considers poverty a problem to be solved, the metrics utilized by it sharply depart from that of bottom-billion capitalism. I was reminded of this divergence repeatedly during the several years that I researched the different worlds of microfinance. At training workshops sponsored by the World Bank and USAID, microfinance practitioners were trained in best practices derived from the world of conventional banking, which was an irony because microfinance was meant to serve as a radical alternative to mainstream finance. Preaching the revolutionary nature of financial markets, experts disseminated risk-assessment methods and frameworks to evaluate financial sustainability. In an industry claiming to serve the bottom billion, there were no metrics to measure the impact of financial inclusion on poverty. By contrast, in the organizations based in Bangladesh, I found robust indicators of vulnerability and social impact, the assessment of poverty, and the assessment of poverty alleviation. Most of all, I found multiple processes of knowledge production, including processes that performed the econometric evaluations most favored by the international development community, as well as rich ethnographies of lives led in poverty and complex archives of institutional struggles against landlords, political bosses, and patriarchs. Not easily formatted in the familiar and recognized frames of global poverty, these stories and histories are still waiting to be recovered, interpreted, and narrated. They have the potential to shift our attention from simplistic solutions to poverty, which are often market-based, to the difficult and necessary work of building pro-poor institutions.

The Ethics and Politics of Voluntarism

On any given day, my email inbox fills up with hopeful messages of social change. I am enlisted to pledge support, via crowd-funding websites, for various world-changing volunteer activities: those that will help orphans in Cambodia or educate poor girls in Nepal or build houses for poor villages in the Philippines or provide toilets to slums in Kenya. Each cause is noble; each argument for how such an intervention will improve the lives of the poor is inspiring; each appeal for crowdfunding seems worthy of support. If the portals of bottom-billion capitalism put on visual display the many opportunities to underwrite the heroic entrepreneurship of the global poor, then the portals of transnational voluntarism seek to crowd-fund the poverty action of eager millennials. This distinctive mode of charity enlists donors, not in giving to the poor but rather in giving to the foot soldiers of poverty action, who in turn promise to transform the lives of the poor. The consequences are profound. On the one hand, poverty comes to be framed as a problem that can be solved through individual acts of liberal benevolence. On the other hand, these intimate encounters with poverty become the crucible in which global citizens, especially those with the privilege and leisure to participate in voluntarism, craft a sense of self and a place in the world.

It is perhaps not surprising that such forms of poverty action have proliferated. After all, in the context of tremendous global and national inequalities of income and wealth, philanthropy has reappeared as a solution
to the problem of poverty. But this is not just any kind of philanthropy.
Called "philanthrocapitalism" (Bishop and Green 2008), it is a social mission for capitalism and a mandate for efficiency and self-sufficiency for
philanthropy. The reliance on philanthropy is ironic given the well-estab-
lished fact, through the research of psychologist Paul Piff, for example,
that the wealthy suffer from a "compassion deficit" and are much less
charitable than the poor (Warner 2010). Yet it is within this matrix of
ideas and practices that millennials pitch their latest volunteer enterprise,
thereby replicating the logic of venture philanthropy and its purported
solutions for global poverty. With this in mind, it is worth staging a shift
in vocabulary from "volunteerism" to "voluntarism" to uncover how the
practice of volunteering becomes a philosophy of private assistance and
poor relief.

An important aspect of voluntarism—or venture philanthropy—is its
temporality. It is deployed with urgency, but as a temporary measure. In
this way, it renders the problem of poverty finite and, most important,
solvable. Not surprisingly, voluntary poverty action proliferates in contexts of emergency—for example, in the aftermath of natural disasters,
such as the catastrophic earthquake in Haiti in 2010 and the super storm
Hurricane Katrina, which devastated New Orleans in 2005. Volunteers
flocked to both sites to assist with reconstruction and to provide humanitarian aid. From short-term church missions to high school service learning trips, post-disaster Haiti and New Orleans became ground zero for
millennial voluntarism. In the absence of sustained government assistance, such volunteer forces have often been the only recourse for recovery,
especially for poor communities. As analyzed by anthropologist Vincanne
Adams (2013) in her provocative book *Markets of Sorrow, Labors of Faith*,
these forms of voluntarism must be understood as an "affect economy,"
mobilizing unpaid (or self-funded or crowd-funded) labor through an
emotional sense of urgency prompted by the tragedy of natural disaster.
Such mobilizations, she notes, are a key component of the overall privatization of disaster relief and the increasing reliance on marketized models
of assistance and recovery.

It is important to disrupt the temporalities of the affect economy and thereby the bounded finitude of poverty as a problem waiting to be solved by well-meaning volunteers. Such disruption is especially important for the case of seemingly natural disasters, where the extraordinary episode of a storm or earthquake masks the invisible and long-standing disasters of social exclusion and spatial segregation that render poor communities uniquely vulnerable to such crises. Thus, geographer Neil Smith (2006, 1) boldly states that "there is no such thing as a natural disaster," claiming, "in every phase and aspect of a disaster—causes, vulnerability, prepared-ness, results and response, and reconstruction—the contours of disaster and the difference between who lives and who dies is to a greater or lesser extent a social calculus." The urgency of a natural disaster not only obscures this social calculus but also creates unprecedented opportunities for unregulated exploitation, predation, and profit, what Naomi Klein (2010) has called "disaster capitalism." Such a state of emergency prolongs rather than mitigates human suffering. This has been the case for poor communities that were displaced by Hurricane Katrina and ignored by the recovery industry. In an interview conducted by Adams (2009), one such displaced resident provides a poignant narrative of this prolonged suffering: "Well, it's kind of like a hamster's wheel. You keep spinning, but you are trying to reach the end of your destination in terms of a job, a home, resources, rebuilding, but you are not getting anywhere. You are in that spinning wheel, you know, but you keep trying. You get up and you go to this place, and you go to this place. . . . Life keeps going on, you see, it's like it's going on, but it's not going on." Contrast this temporality of endless waiting with narratives of venturesome voluntarism: "New Orleans is the perfect voluntourism destination and offers hundreds of opportunities to help. . . . If you're in New Orleans for a day or more, you can get your hands in the dirt and help directly with some gardening. . . . Volunteers go directly to residents' homes to install energy-efficient lightbulbs, so this opportunity is perfect for anyone visiting the city, even if for just a few hours" (Schwietert 2008). Of course, not all types of voluntarism take the absurd temporal form of a few hours or a few days. But what is at stake here is the uneasy fit between sustained human suffering and episodic intervention, between the trauma of the ever-spinning hamster's wheel and the optimism of the crowdfunded volunteer venture that promises immediate results. Indeed, my students provide thoughtful auto-critiques of their own roles as volunteers—during spring break in New Orleans, in architecture studios that spend a week in Haiti. For example, many are drawn to Ivan Illich's controversial speech "To Hell with Good Intentions," which he delivered to the Conference on InterAmerican Student Projects in Mexico in 1968:

> @*audge_podge1* #GlobalPOV "Next to money and guns, the third largest North American export is the U.S. idealist . . . the volunteer . . . "- Ivan Illich

Others simply find their own language of critique:

> @*MissSilva3* Volunteerism, voluntarism, voluntourism, volunterrorism . . . #globalpov

Voluntarism of course is not new. In his magisterial social history of welfare in America, *In the Shadow of the Poorhouse*, historian Michael Katz describes how, at key historical moments in U.S. cities, when poverty had become sharply visible and the limits of poor relief had been reached, a recurring mode of charity—friendly visiting—emerged and re-emerged. Whether a part of antebellum voluntarism, the scientific charity organizations of the 1870s, or the settlement houses of the late nineteenth century, friendly visitors have "diagnosed the great social problem of the day as the chasm that had opened between classes, which it proposed to close through human contact" (Katz 1986, 70). Prevalent structural inequalities, such as exploitative conditions of work, were usually ignored. Such forms of poverty action were also often fiercely opposed to public assistance for the poor, viewing welfare not as a right but rather as a private act of charity that well-to-do classes would deliver to paupers. Yet Katz also reminds us of the rare moments of rupture during which this consensus on poverty and charity would unravel. Take, for example, the settlement movement that swept through American cities in the 1890s. The movement, which was largely made up of idealistic college graduates, soon became a space of "research and activism" (Katz 1986, 164). A departure from friendly visiting, it involved members of the middle-class moving into settlement houses that were established in poor neighborhoods. Indeed, proponents of the movement saw "settlement in the slums" as "an outpost of education and culture" (Katz 1986, 164). The settlement movement provided new career paths and professional opportunities for young Americans, especially women. Katz (1986, 166) writes: "Largely excluded from law, medicine, business, and the ministry, only school-teaching, nursing, perhaps working in a library, or charity remained as occupations suitable for respectable young women. Settlements offered an exciting option: an unparalleled chance to work for worthwhile ends in the company of other educated, sympathetic women." The settlement movement also transformed, if only for a brief moment, the frames of poverty that otherwise dominated public debate and action in America. In particular, residence in the slums seemed to catalyze middle-class support for working-class struggles, labor unions, and involvement in various policy and legislative battles such as "statewide tenement house reform, child labor laws, regulations governing the working conditions of women, factory inspection, and women's suffrage" (Katz 1986, 166). Many settlement workers went on to have prominent careers in public service and politics, helping craft important parts of the New Deal, promoting grassroots progressivism, and eventually forming an "aggressive 'new middle class' of experts that tried to transform virtually every facet of American life" (Katz 1986, 174).

This brief historical reflection reveals the recurrence of voluntarism as a means of mediating poverty, inequality, and the chasm of social class. Yet it is worth considering the moments at which such encounters with poverty become what Lawson and Elwood (2014) call "contact zones," which they define as "boundary-breaking, transformative moments" that "lead to new negotiations of identity, privilege, political responsibility and alliance." The settlement movement seems to have been one such moment, transforming friendly visiting into residence in slums and shifting poverty action from the intimacies of personal charity to policy and legislative battles against structural inequality. Are similar moments possible in today's age of poverty? Several years ago, the United Nations Human Development Report (Fukuda-Parr 2003, 144) argued that "policy, not charity" is what rich countries can do to help achieve the Millennium Development Goals. Can today's voluntarism impress such an adage upon eager millennials? The case of ethical consumerism is an interesting example of the efforts being made to shift policy.

As noted earlier, ethical consumerism is a set of ideas and practices that enable empowered global citizens to act on the problem of poverty through consumption choices. In its crudest form, it suggests that we can shop our way to the end of poverty. Yet ethical consumerism can also be understood as a terrain of struggle, one that transforms individual and personal acts of consumption into confrontations with structures of global inequality. With this in mind, our students ponder the value chains of global commodities, such as coffee. They slowly but surely trace the origins of an over-priced cappuccino brewed by a Berkeley barista to the poverty-stricken lives of coffee farmers in Ethiopia. We then watch them stomp out of the classroom with the resolve never to drink a cup of coffee again, some of them on their cell phones calling their friends and parents to garner similar pledges of boycott. As we cover the history of other commodities—from colonial tea plantations to neocolonial banana plantations—the students come to realize that there is no escape from complicity in global consumption. And when we discuss the cut flower industry, they are faced with the difficult reality that our most sentimental celebrations, from Valentine's Day to Mother's Day, rely on the invisible labor of underpaid workers—often women—living under conditions of poverty. But it is this anguish of the ethical consumer that leads them to actively pursue more information about campaigns such as fair trade. Not satisfied with simply purchasing a cup of fair trade coffee at the local café, they immerse themselves in learning about how fair trade seeks to create more equitable terms of trade for small producers and farmer cooperatives. In doing so, they inevitably run up against the powerful institutions through which the global market economy is planned—that system of "extreme artificiality," as Polanyi would put it. Once only concerned with ethical choices while shopping at Gap or buying produce at Whole Foods Market, these millennials must now consider the highly unequal rules, tariffs, subsidies, and protections through which trade is structured. The World Trade Organization comes into view. U.S. agro-subsidies, buttressed by entrenched political lobbies, become visible. The global market is no longer a decentralized system of producers and consumers making rational, individual choices. Instead, it appears as monopolistic power, maintained through various forms of what Polanyi once called "interventionism." Acting upon poverty, these students come to acknowledge, might require something different than the affective

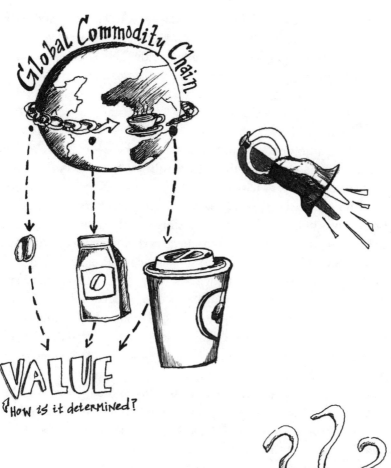

Global Commodity Chain

VALUE
How is it determined?

practices of voluntarism and the ethics of doing good. Thinking and acting against the hamster's wheel of inequality, these global citizens come to realize, might require a timeline quite different than an alternative spring break or a summer of service-learning.

Poor People's Movements

I am an urbanist. My interest in cities is shaped by the indelible experience of my childhood years in the city of my birth, Kolkata, India. One of the world's infamous megacities, Kolkata is a place of considerable poverty, and its slums are rife with iconic images of human suffering. Of course, this was not how I knew the city. My middle-class life played out in a different urban world. I received a prim and proper school education, my classmates and I always dressed in starched and pleated uniforms, polished patent leather shoes, and white socks pulled up to our knees; my family lived in a modest home, but it was kept clean amid the dirt and debris of the city by domestic workers; we had a ramshackle Ambassador car, but it was driven by the "family chauffeur," which ensured that I would not have to navigate the city's overcrowded and dilapidated public transportation system.

After getting a college education in the United States, I returned to Kolkata with a new purpose: doctoral research. This led me to study a city that lay outside of my familiar world, a city of persistent poverty and deprivation. I discovered the complex political negotiations through which the urban poor found a foothold in the city, their only option, often, being to squat—always tenuously—along railway tracks and filthy water canals. I traced the daily lives of poor women from neighboring villages as they poured into the city every morning on local trains to sell vegetables and clean homes. I bore witness to evictions and demolitions as the city sought to remake itself as a hub of global investment by displacing the settlements and livelihoods of the poor. In Kolkata, I learned not only about poverty but also about the *urban* character of such poverty.

In a set of important philosophical interventions, Henri Lefebvre argues that, just as the world was once transformed by an industrial revolution, so it is now being transformed by an urban revolution. Lefebvre ([1974] 1991) is concerned not with a spatial type (i.e., the city) but rather with what he describes as the "production of space"—the buying, selling, and exchange of parts of space through which global capitalism comes to be animated and vitalized. Take, for instance, the spectacles of urban development and gentrification that are unfolding worldwide, creating skyrocketing economic value for real estate in cities such as Manhattan and Mumbai. Take, for instance, the global formula of the "world-class city," which pits city against city in a competition to build extravagant infrastructure for global elites: world-class airports connecting to world-class expressways that serve world-class gated communities, world-class shopping malls, and world-class golf courses, all financed by debt at world-class interest rates.

The #GlobalPOV Project, *Are Slums the Global Urban Future?*
www.youtube.com/watch?v=1xk7dr3VG6s

But Lefebvre ([1974] 1991) also reminds us that space is social, and while it is a means of domination and power, it can also be appropriated for human needs. It is this social meaning of space, its "use-value" rather than its "exchange-value," which undergirds Lefebvre's concept of the "right to the city." A rallying cry for urban social movements around the world, the right to the city is, as scholars have noted, a capacious concept: it is "not only a right to *habitat* (as the UN conferences have largely interpreted it) or *La Fête* (the ability to participate in the spectacle and shape it to new ends, a primary concern of Lefebvre), but also a right to the *oeuvre* (the ability to participate in the *work* and the *making* of the city) and the right to urban life (which is to say the right to be *part* of the city—to be present, *to be*)" (Mitchell and Heynen 2009, 616).

In the age of poverty, there are numerous efforts to solve the problem of urban poverty. From slum-upgrading programs to safe water and sanitation schemes, the megacity is a key site at which the technical interventions of human development are feverishly being implemented. Also present are the interlocutors of bottom-billion capitalism, who view the urban poor as ingenious entrepreneurs and slums as economic workhorses. Their solutions for urban poverty involve providing access to credit and collateral to the poor, thereby capitalizing these economies at the "bottom of the pyramid." But if we are to think with Lefebvre, then it becomes difficult to sustain the notion of urban poverty as a problem that can be solved. Instead, we must consider, as geographer David Harvey (2008, 40) notes, "the question of who commands the necessary connection between urbanization and surplus production and use." With such a question, we have reached the limits of popular and prevalent modes of poverty action, be it the ladder of development, bottom-billion capitalism, or voluntarism. But such a question is central to the struggles of poor people's movements, many of them organized around the concept of the "right to the city." I borrow the term "poor people's movements" from the classic text by sociologists Frances Fox Piven and Richard Cloward about social mobilizations in the United States to pinpoint struggles that are organized and led by the poor within the broader gamut of social dissent. Piven and Cloward (1977, x) call for a "dialectical analysis" of poor people's movements such that they are understood not as a radical rupture with the status quo but instead as "both formed by and directed against institutional arrangements." Here is a glimpse of some poor people's movements that are seeking to challenge the social and spatial relations of inequality so starkly apparent in cities around the world.

On the edges of Kolkata, the construction of the Indian "world-class city" has been blocked by fierce mobilizations of peasants, sharecroppers, and squatters. Rallying against land grabs by the state for purposes of setting up industrial enclaves and special economic zones, such movements challenge the premise that development requires the displacement and dispossession of the poor (Roy 2011). These struggles are not new. In India, the National Alliance of People's Movements (NAPM) has been battling myriad dispossessions enacted in the name of development—from large dams to urban infrastructure projects—since the 1990s. Thus, activist and writer Arundhati Roy (2001, 71) begins her poignant essay "The Greater Common Good" by quoting former Indian prime minister and ardent advocate of modernization Jawaharlal Nehru: "If you are to suffer, you should suffer in the interest of the country." Nehru made this statement in 1948 to villagers displaced by a dam. As Roy notes, such projects sacrifice the poor and powerless in the name of the "greater common good"—although this is a good that, for them, never arrives. Taking stock of the achievements of India, the world's largest democracy, she concludes: "Already fifty million people have been fed into the Development Mill and have emerged as air-conditioners and popcorn and rayon suits—*subsidised* air-conditioners and popcorn and rayon suits (if we must have these nice things, and they *are* nice, at least we should be made to pay for them)." Roy's essay was written to express solidarity with the Narmada Bachao Andalan, a social movement affiliated with the NAPM and organized to stop the building of the Sardar Sarovar Dam on the Narmada river, a project financed by the World Bank. In an unprecedented move, the World Bank withdrew its funding for the project in 1993, citing human and environmental costs. Roy (2001, 97) wrote: "No one has ever managed to make the World Bank step back from a project before. Least of all a rag-tag army of the poorest people in one of the world's poorest countries." Indeed, the Narmada protests had far-reaching impacts on how the World Bank itself evaluates the costs and benefits of development projects. However, the construction of the dam continued, with financing from the government of Gujarat.

On the edges of Chicago, amid foreclosed homes and abandoned communities, the Chicago Anti-Eviction Campaign seeks to appropriate space for human needs. When Martha Biggs, a mother of four, was evicted from public housing, she found herself homeless, sleeping in the family's minivan. The Chicago Anti-Eviction Campaign found shelter for her by occupying, reclaiming, and rehabbing a foreclosed house. In doing so, they created a place for Biggs and her children to call home (figure 3.2). But they also crafted a methodology of shelter activism, one that pivots on an elegant idea: "homeless people in peopleless homes."

As described by journalist Laura Gottesdiener (2013), such appropriations must be understood in a broader context—the devastations wrought by predatory subprime lending and subsequent home foreclosures in U.S. cities, especially in African-American neighborhoods. Her account of "evictions at gunpoint" in Chicago remind us that brutal displacements and violent dispossessions take place in the global North as often as they do in the global South. If poor people's movements in India have

Figure 3.2. Martha Biggs in her new home in Chicago. (Photograph by Brent Lewis.)

sought to make visible how the poor are sacrificed in the name of development, then in the United States, community organizing groups such as
the Chicago Anti-Eviction Campaign demonstrate the "sacrifice zones"
of American urbanization. To appropriate space in these sacrifice zones
is to remake the city itself. Yet, following Piven and Cloward, such
movements must be understood as "both formed by and directed
against institutional arrangements." Urban homesteader movements,
including the Chicago Anti-Eviction Campaign, simultaneously contest
and deploy notions of property, legitimizing the occupation of foreclosed
homes through practices of beautification and improvement. They thus
challenge the absurdity of homelessness amid a sea of peopleless homes,
but the basis of the challenge often rests on principles of propertied
citizenship.

Perhaps the most ambitious experiments with new institutional arrangements of urbanism have taken place recently in Brazil. Urban reform

movements, often cross-class coalitions, unfolded alongside Brazil's transition to democracy and enshrined the right to the city in the Citizen Constitution of 1988. Paralleling other prominent efforts to tackle sociospatial inequality (such as movements of the rural landless, notably the Movimento dos Trabalhadores Sem Terra—the Landless Worker's Movement) as well as experiments with local democracy (for example, participatory budgeting in the city of Porto Alegre), a new regime of "participatory urban planning" was created and institutionalized through the 2001 City Statute. Hailed by urbanists Teresa Caldeira and James Holston (2014, 4) as a "remarkable law" and a "democratic project of great ambition," this legislative framework asserts the role of the state in managing and realizing the social functions of cities, especially the social function of property. The statute also entails a democratization of the process of urban planning, requiring master plans to be formulated through processes of popular participation. Equally significant, the City Statute expresses the right to the city as a collective right, thereby providing an alternative to the traditions of legal liberalism entrenched in the Brazilian code that had, up until the statute was enacted, defined individual rights. The City Statute must be seen as the culmination of decades of struggle by poor people's movements. But as Caldeira and Holston (2014, 13) note, the politics of "working-class citizens" cannot be contained within the "institutionalized spaces of mandated participation." Also evident in Brazil is how fragile the right to the city is, even when that right has been institutionalized as law. For instance, when Brazilian cities, from Rio de Janeiro to Sao Paulo, host world-class sporting events, such as the World Cup and the Olympics, the poor are once again violently displaced to make way for forms of urban development from which they will garner negligible benefit. The sacrifice zones appear even within the people's democracy.

The Chicago Anti-Eviction Campaign draws its inspiration from the Western Cape Anti-Eviction Campaign, which was formed in 2000 in South Africa with the aim of fighting evictions, water cutoffs, and poor health services, obtaining free electricity, securing decent housing, and opposing police brutality. Thus, a poor people's movement in the global

South served as the template for an organization that arranges housing takeovers in Chicago's suburban fringe. Indeed, it is in the cities of the global South that collective action by the urban poor has become an important platform of social justice. Anthropologist Arjun Appadurai (2002) has labeled such poor people's movements "deep democracy" and drawn attention to the horizontal ties of solidarity through which they constitute global formations of protest, knowledge, and mobilization. Particularly important are the ways in which such South-North alliances connect contemporary dispossession in cities like Chicago to the long histories of colonialism and imperialism in places like South Africa. In 2009, the Western Cape Anti-Eviction Campaign published an open letter to U.S. activists in *The Nation:*

> The privatization of land—a public resource for all that has now become a false commodity—was the original sin, the original cause of this financial crisis. With the privatization of land comes the dispossession of people from their land which was held in common by communities. With the privatization of land comes the privatization of everything else, because once land can be bought and sold, almost anything else can eventually be bought and sold.
>
> As the poor of South Africa, we know this because we live it. Colonialism and apartheid dispossessed us of our land and gave it to whites to be bought and sold for profit. When apartheid as a systematic racial instrument ended in 1994, we did not get our land back. . . .
>
> So, in 1999, 2000 and 2001, farms, townships, ghettos and shack settlements all across South Africa erupted against evictions, water cutoffs, electricity cutoffs and the like. We have been fighting for small things and small issues, but our communities are also fighting two larger battles.
>
> The first is embodied in the declaration we make to the outside world: We may be poor but we are not stupid! We may be poor, but we can still think! Nothing for us without us! Talk to us, not about us! We are fighting for democracy. The right to be heard and the right to be in control of our own communities and our own society. . . .
>
> Second, while our actions may seem like a demand for welfare couched in a demand for houses, social grants and water, they are actually a demand to end the commodification of things that cannot be commodified: land, labour and money.

I share this excerpt because it provides an important glimpse of the capacity of poor people's movements to articulate a sophisticated transnational and historical analysis of dispossession. If you are reminded of Lefebvre or Polanyi in reading the passage, then it should serve as a reminder that the poor "are not stupid," that they too are theorists of global capitalism. The Western Cape Anti-Eviction Campaign boldly states that the terrain of struggle lies not in securing shelter or services but instead in enacting democratic politics and decommodification. Several other urban social movements in South Africa share this vision, notably Abahlali baseMjondolo, a shackdwellers' movement fighting against forced removals and for housing, education, and popular democracy. Political theorist Richard Pithouse notes that Abahlali baseMjondolo has made efforts to create a space of radical autonomy, for example, by refusing electoral participation, rejecting NGO vanguardism, and creating alternative economies, such as those based on commoning. Yet, as Pithouse (2014, 142) points out, the state cannot be so easily ignored: "It is only via the state that spatial inclusion can be secured and the surplus redistributed via social projects. If we reduced our thinking of the urban question to the commons, we would be left with occupied land—some of it constituting spatial insurgency—vegetable gardens and so on but no way to think beyond survivalism or gradual inclusion and into real transformation of both the material quality of people's lives and the nature of South African cities."

GOVERNING POVERTY

In this chapter, we have outlined how poverty is governed as a global problem. Drawing on the iconic debate between two development economists, Jeffrey Sachs and William Easterly, we argue that dominant frames of poverty knowledge and action run up against two stubborn puzzles: the puzzle of markets and the puzzle of colonialism. Both of these are in fact part of the same puzzle, that of the relationship between capitalism and poverty. This relationship, as we noted in the previous chapter, is the most significant dilemma that haunts the age of global poverty and interrupts the optimism of its foot soldiers. The three problem-spaces discussed in this chapter—microfinance, post-disaster intervention, and urban poverty—highlight this dilemma. But they also reveal various practices and discourses that imagine and build institutions, legal frameworks, and movements that confront and challenge the relationship between capitalism and poverty. A key part of this work is a reframing of poverty, both of poor others and of poverty expertise. I provide here two examples from my recent public scholarship of such reframing, one concerned with the trope of dependent poor others and the other concerned with the theory of social change associated with poverty expertise.

Coda 1: Reframing Dependency

An enduring paradox lies at the heart of the world-class city. World-class cities, everywhere alike, are built by the poor. Slum dwellers, squatters, day laborers, informal vendors, migrant workers—these are the people whose hands construct the shimmering towers of the world-class city, raise its children, clean its villas and penthouses. They constitute the urban majority of world-class cities. Yet cities aspiring to be world-class— to be just like every other world-class city—tend to expel this urban majority, literally erasing their presence from the face of the city. World-class urbanism declares as nuisance and filth, and thus disposable, those who are in fact essential to the world-class city.

As an urbanist, I have sought to make visible these relations of dependency, demonstrating how prosperous urban lifestyles depend on the labor of the poor. There is quite a bit at stake in such reframings of dependency. Take the case of India. There, in 2000, a landmark ruling by the country's supreme court defined the slum dweller as an "encroacher," usurping public land "for private use free of cost." To provide assistance or resettlement to slum dwellers, the court concluded, was akin to "giving a reward to a pickpocket" (Bhan 2009, 135). Such a framing obscures the role of the urban poor as city-builders but also obscures the various encroachments and usurpations of urban elites that escape criminalization or even scrutiny.

In their seminal article "A Genealogy of *Dependency*," feminist theorists Nancy Fraser and Linda Gordon expose how, in the United States, poverty has been reframed as a problem of welfare dependency. This means not only that the poor are burdened with stigma but also that poverty itself comes to be seen as "individual problems, as much moral or psychological as economic" (Fraser and Gordon 1994, 311). Indeed, the systematic erosion of the U.S. welfare state, which started in the Reagan presidency and continued into the heyday of the Clinton presidency, pivoted on the stereotype of the "welfare queen"—inevitably imagined as a black single mother—who scammed taxpayers through welfare fraud schemes and squandered her public assistance money on alcohol and drugs. Yet as social work scholar Mimi Abramovitz (2001, 299) has argued, it is crucial to recognize that there are many dimensions of the U.S. welfare system— social, fiscal, and corporate—and that welfare programs "generally favor middle and upper-income groups over low-income groups." These hidden welfare benefits include tax deductions for home mortgages, tax breaks for the affluent, and subsidies for corporations.

With this in mind, I like to replace Easterly's line, "the rich have markets, the poor have bureaucrats," with the line, "the rich have state-help, the poor have self-help." In our controversial and widely viewed #GlobalPOV video, *Who is Dependent on Welfare?*, we conclude that America's welfare queen is the Walmart Corporation, its massive corporate profits enabled by the low wages it pays its workforce, a large proportion of which must rely on Medicaid and food stamp assistance. In a rejoinder, *Forbes* columnist Carrie Sheffield (2014) labels the video "agit-prop," dismisses poor people's movements as "crowd rage and mobocracy," and argues that "food stamps are not a sustainable solution to poverty, and arbitrarily expanding the welfare state has unintended negative consequences, including incentivizing unwed births." Her statement is a telling glimpse of dominant frames of poverty and dependency in the world's (for now) most prosperous country.

The #GlobalPOV Project, *Who is Dependent on Welfare?*
www.youtube.com/watch?v=-rtySUhuokM

But, as the welfare state has been dismantled in the global North, ambitious experiments with social protection and welfare have been launched in the global South. Indeed, as structural adjustment and austerity take hold in the North Atlantic and futures of social democracy seem foreclosed, governments in the so-called developing world are undertaking massive programs of social inclusion. Some of these programs, such as conditional cash transfer schemes, which provide means-tested cash grants to poor households on the condition that education and health targets are met, continue key themes of previous regimes of development. As sociologist Maxine Molyneux has shown, these programs deploy principles of participation, coresponsibility, and empowerment and depend on the active role of poor women in achieving development outcomes. She thus provocatively asks if these new poverty agendas are a case of "female altruism at the service of the state" (Molyneux 2006). Yet conditional cash transfers have also been hailed as a new social contract between the poor and government. In countries like Brazil, the program is more appropriately understood as an *un*conditional cash transfer, with millions of poor households receiving cash grants with few behavioral conditions. In a fascinating interview conducted by geographers Jamie Peck and Nik Theodore (2015), a member of the World Bank team in Brasilia explained the importance of cash transfers in this way: "[Here], the poor are poor because of a historical process of social exclusion, and we owe them a debt. That's fundamental in Brazilian thinking: they have citizens' rights [but] have not always had access to those rights, and we have to pay this debt back to the poor. . . . Their view is . . . if I have a child not attending school [but on the] program, are we going to take it [the allowance] away? Is my first response a penalty or a punishment? No, our response should be to go and investigate, to use it as a flag—use it as a flag for *more care*. For them, they would say that the C, as in CCT [conditional cash transfer], is for care." Such formulations move us away from stereotypes of the welfare dependency of the poor to conceptualizations of the social debt of governments to their people. It is thus that organizations struggling for a global basic income, such as the Basic Income Earth Network, make the case for a universal and unconditional minimum income that would be paid by the state to all members of a political community, without means tests or work requirements. This, argues development studies scholar Guy Standing (2014), is a key part of a charter for the world's "precariat."

Coda 2: Why I Became an Urban Planner

Many years ago, as I completed a self-designed undergraduate degree in Comparative Urban Studies at a small liberal-arts college in the United States, I made the decision to pursue a graduate degree in urban planning. My passion was to understand urban poverty and inequality and to make social change. As a discipline and profession, urban planning gave me many ways of encountering the problem of poverty. I could place the problem within the long history of techno-scientific modernization and search for solutions. I could situate the problem within utopian visions of a better society, those that have sought to create alternative economies and alternative communities. More recently though, I have come to place the question (rather than problem) of urban poverty in the unfinished business of the freedom struggles of the twentieth century.

Ananya Roy at TEDCity2.0, September 2013, "Exploring the Ingenuity of the World's Most Vulnerable" www.tedcity2.org/talks/exploring-the-ingenuity-of-the-worlds-most-vulnerable/

Let me explain by sharing a moment from a visit to South Africa. In 2013, I had the privilege of giving a talk at Witwatersrand University in Johannesburg in memory of an anti-apartheid activist and architect, Lionel "Rusty" Bernstein. On the morning of the talk, I accompanied some of the students and faculty to Kliptown, a district of Soweto, on the outskirts of Johannesburg. Kliptown is the site of South Africa's famed Freedom Charter, the 1955 charter that envisioned the end of apartheid. It was an extraordinary statement of equality and social justice, and Rusty Bernstein, among others, was a signatory. There is now a monument in Kliptown commemorating the Freedom Charter, complete with a luxury hotel that has a bar named after Rusty, which offers a signature cocktail,

Figure 3.3. A shack in Kliptown, Johannesburg. (Photograph by Ananya Roy.)

the Kliptini (although Rusty's daughter told me that her father rarely drank alcohol). But less than half a mile from the monument is this: the shacks of the urban majority (figure 3.3). We were given a tour of the area by Robert, a man who diligently keeps a notebook of all visitors and who generously tells the story of each humiliation, each deprivation, and each eviction (figure 3.4).

I came of political age during the anti-apartheid movement; that struggle defined my generation as it defined the closing decades of the twentieth century. When apartheid ended, it seemed that the dream of freedom movements, from anticolonialism to civil rights, had been fulfilled. But my generation was wrong. The shacks of Kliptown tell us otherwise. Virtually invisible in the shadow of the African world-class city of Johannesburg, they suggest that there is unfinished business. This is not the problem of poverty waiting to be solved through a new generation of poverty experts, social entrepreneurs, and well-meaning volunteers. It is the difficult and

Figure 3.4. Robert giving a tour of the Kliptown shacks.
(Photograph by Ananya Roy.)

unending work of social and spatial justice. Social justice is not a governable problem, it is a demand. We, the experts, do not decide who gets which model or which version or which portion of social justice. Instead, we have the privilege of participating in the collective labor of thinking and acting against inequality.

4 Modeling Poverty

Kweku Opoku-Agyemang

A DILEMMA TALE

Once upon a time,
When the world was young,
In the very first village,
Was the very first argument,
Because the world was young.
Two women, Aba and Abena, were engaged in a deep quarrel.
"This land is mine!"
"No, it is mine!"
Until they called the elders to settle the issue,
Because elders are able to do such things.
The elders hosted the first sleeping competition,
Which is exactly what it sounds like:
The one who sleeps the longest wins.
"Ready, set sleep!"
Watching people sleep is not that exciting, so people went to find more
    interesting things to do.
When they returned at sunset, they noticed Aba had rolled off her mat.
Following the tracks, they saw her afloat and being pulled by the tide.
"Aba! Wake up!" To no avail, alas.
People started to head back,

Only to find Abena had rolled off her mat as well,
Into the mysterious forest.
There she was, still asleep,
Surrounded by the fiercest of mosquitoes.
The swarm was so thick you couldn't see through them.
"Abena! Wake up!" To no avail, alas.
And she kept rolling, but the mosquitoes didn't seem to be complaining.
People started to head back,
Only to find both Aba and Abena
Back in the village, each back on her mat,
Still asleep,
Fast asleep.
Obviously, this didn't work, so the elders decided to wake them up with an
   akyeampong leaf.
They both woke up
At the same time,
Still mad, and the quarrel ensued.
The elders want to know,
Because you seem like someone who would know,
Who should get the land and why?

Growing up in Ghana, my father and mother would tell my siblings, cousins, and I such *dilemma tales,* also called *judgment tales.* We would get even more stories in primary school, and we would tirelessly debate how the story should end while the narrator would look on with a smile, refusing to give much more information beyond, "I don't know, what do *you* think and *why?*" Common in many African and other countries, a dilemma tale is a useful device for developing argumentative skills. The narrative is disciplined by the relatively simple and admittedly unrealistic universe provided by a story. The origins of allegorical folklore traditions in the precolonial African era are imprecise, but their ability to simulate legal institutions (noted in the example) may help explain their regularity and endurance. Cognitively, a dilemma tale balances two competing needs: resolution and difference.

The above tale imposes on its audience themes of economics and politics. Land is one of the most important economic resources, and countless wars and other political contests have happened around land through the centuries. These two areas, economics and politics, have influenced my own thinking on development.

All Ghanaian public university graduates are given, despite all the system's shortcomings, an outstanding and tuition-free education. In return, all graduates must complete a year-long internship called National Service. Most graduates prefer to refer to it as National *Slavery,* since attempting to reconcile an academic identity of comfortable abstraction with the reality of poverty is often a humbling experience. After earning my bachelor's degree in Economics with Geography and Resource Development, I served my National Service year with a government group that was working to lower HIV/AIDS prevalence rates among poor youth who were struggling to remain in school. Working with policymakers taught me to ask better questions, and the poverty question led me to the United States for graduate school. I studied economics at Ohio University in Athens, Ohio, under phenomenal mentorship. Athens was one of the poorest counties in Ohio, and it was jarring to see the poverty's utter lack of reverence for boundaries.

After completing my degree in Athens, I enrolled in the Development Studies PhD program at the University of Wisconsin-Madison, taking classes in economics, political science, history, anthropology, and sociology. I gravitated toward political economy and a main specialization in economics. Graduate training in the political economics of development provided me with an excellent setting to grapple with the question of global poverty, and I left with many skills in my toolkit—even if none of them had completely solved my global poverty quandary. When I was reunited with my parents at graduation, they and my many non-economist friends wanted to know more about what I did and how I did it. I was excited to share, but I found that it was not easy to use the level of detail I wanted to. More recently, the reason for this hit me: development economics in particular, and science and development in general, is to some extent a special case of a dilemma tale.

This chapter discusses the economics of global poverty in the form of dilemma tales. This approach necessarily departs from the prevalent scientific model framework from which I continue to benefit. Thomas Kuhn (1962), perhaps the greatest philosopher of science, understood that instead of a higher authority mediating scientific claims, what actually happened in many instances of knowledge progress was that scholars escaped the skin within which they conducted their research. One ambition of the chapter is to help fellow economists do and benefit from this. The audience of the chapter, however, is not exclusively economics researchers.

Understanding economics perspectives is increasingly important for emerging students and policy makers who are concerned with global poverty. Economics is a useful lens through which to view global poverty because there are few to no exceptions to the subject access afforded by an economics orientation. To illustrate, economics has successfully covered nearly every topic directly or indirectly related to poverty, including conflict, charity, organ transplants, love, war, and beauty (to name but a few), *in addition* to the traditional national economy.

Economists' agendas are inherently ambitious. If physics tries to develop a theory of *everything*, then economics attempts to come up with a theory of *everyone*. This affords economics a sense of ease when entering other social science fields, whether political science, sociology, history, or anthropology. A simplistic illustrative analogy to explain how this works draws on mobile software. A good metaphor for economics is Apple's App Store. Unlike Google's Android platform, to which most software app programmers can contribute, the App Store mandates that all new apps be rigorously subjected to Apple's preordained but slowly-evolving ideals of minimalism and simplicity. The trade of ideas often goes in a single direction: from economics into other social sciences, with relatively few exceptions.

Economists' dominance is hence similar to the colonial expansion from which "economic imperialism" psychologically derives, as any colonialist unaffectedly and sincerely finds foreign thought inadequate and thus requiring his modification. Economics now occupies the hegemonic position that Freudian psychiatrists did in the 1950s and that historians and religious priests did long before. Hegemony notwithstanding, it is worth conceding that economics' minimalism is an essential approach to global poverty.

This chapter is motivated by the observation that economics yields a unique understanding of what is "interesting" about poverty. To most people, the word "interesting" implies that an idea is remarkable in and of itself, usually arousing *questions*. In economics, however, "interesting" usually means that an idea is solvable, estimable, and broadly reconcilable with a model for the sake of an *answer*. To meet each audience halfway, this chapter radically merges what both groups consider interesting about global poverty, presenting economic *dilemmas* instead of mere *models*. This approach is necessary because a model requires a sense of *certainty* that a dilemma relinquishes, or even actively *resists*. Many observers and students intuitively sense that *any* certainty about solving poverty requires some scientific assurance. A dilemma tale approach requires a modest orientation to development economics.

How does economic theorizing and modeling—*narrating*—occur in the context of global poverty? If the economics of development is indeed most often a dilemma tale, the story may feel *ruined*, since every reader already knows the dilemma: *How can we know global poverty?*

This chapter proceeds as follows. We first motivate conceptual theories and the evaluative theories used to test them as dilemma tales. We then discuss behavioral economics and the role of measurement in understanding poverty as a dilemma. We go on to examine historical and contextual paradigms as dilemmas with respect to a novel course titled Poverty, Technology, and Development at the University of California, Berkeley, before identifying economists as participants or characters in the stories they themselves create, provoking more dilemmas. The chapter then concludes.

THEORIES AS STORIES

In addition to thinking about an economy as a system or an arrangement, economists mentally construct a household, business, political or social group, or university as resembling an economy, arrangement, or *system*, much in the way that people regularly think of the human body, any ecosystem, or even the solar system as *arrangements*.

Economists use a model or theory to understand or anticipate how a system works. A theory, like any story, forces the storyteller to be specific and openly show his or her assumptions and how they lead to his or her predictions. This is most often done mathematically, but Rubenstein and Osborne (1994) famously noted that many economic theories could be presented plainly, which is a goal this chapter strives for.

Let us consider the stratospheric rise of microfinance—the practice of giving small loans to rural entrepreneurs—which peaked in 2006 when Mohammad Yunus won the Nobel Peace Prize for his momentous work with Grameen Bank. Recently, this success has been complicated by a severe global fallout in the wake of a series of tragic suicides by farmers in India who could not repay their microfinance loans. Our ongoing *dilemma* in the policy-making world is, does microcredit grow businesses in India?

The *system*, in this case, is the social setting that rural Indian citizens find themselves in or are embedded into. We need to create a story that helps us better understand this environment. In a perfect world, each Indian entrepreneur would receive precisely the amount of credit he or she is good for—that is, the amount he or she can successfully repay—and both lender and borrower would be happy. But in the real world, unfortunately, creditors are not very good at identifying creditworthy entrepreneurs—which means credit may make entrepreneurs *worse* off, as shown by the tragedies just mentioned, as lenders often lend wrongly and overburden entrepreneurs.

What is the perspective of an entrepreneur in India? Suppose an entrepreneur in India seeks to borrow funds for a business. For simplicity's sake, let us assume that the business rewards only depend on the ability of the entrepreneur to secure funds, so that these returns depend on how much investment the entrepreneur makes. The entrepreneur could choose to default on the loan once the business is completed. Therefore, the lender must ensure that the borrower has enough "skin in the game," and borrowers will only be able to borrow as much as their independent wealth allows them to. This simple story about the financial system and the challenges creditors face in knowing "who is who" explains why interest rates tend to be extremely high in rural parts of India. This issue is only exacerbated by unregulated, informal moneylenders and lenders' ability to set prices.

Why is this important for *knowing poverty?* Surprisingly, that credit markets are so often imperfect—meaning that clients know more about their own ability and sincerity than their lenders do—is true of most markets. Another example of imperfect markets is labor markets. That is, we could easily think of potential employers as being similar to creditors and potential employees as playing the figurative role of credit customers. This analogy travels, since an employer looking for an employee has a broad perspective that is not entirely different from a creditor looking for a creditworthy customer. Furthermore, just as in the relationship between a creditor and a customer, a potential employer knows *less* about a potential employee than that employee knows about himself or herself. An influential general theory of such lopsided information was created by Joseph Stiglitz and Andrew Weiss (1981) to understand why lenders ration credit, as described above. Similar analogies have been seen in other markets as well.

Analogies are useful for economic narration in general. Many models actually proceed entirely by analogy, so the way farmers adopt new technologies in Ghana could be similar to the way doctors adopt new antibiotics in the United States—their social networks may be similarly important for how the adoption decision is made (Conley and Udry 2010). Just as dilemma tales travel and change in different African countries, many economic models don't technically entirely *belong* to the narrator; they are often tweaked to fit the environment under study.

Every story has, to some extent, been told before.

We return to our story.

What does it mean to be in a system in which lenders cannot tell who is a good risk and who isn't? For us, it means that the story could go either way. Given the challenges of identifying creditworthy entrepreneurs, it is just as possible that entrepreneurs receiving loans become *better* off as it is that they become *worse* off.

The stakes of the story may be even higher. Profits of businesses may change (which is good for the bank), but what about consumption and living standards for the entrepreneur? What about health, education, and women's empowerment? These factors may all benefit from a single loan.

The story proceeds as follows, using the same language as above for transparency:

A poor entrepreneur in India seeks to borrow funds for a business.

The business rewards only depend on the ability of the entrepreneur to secure funds.

This person could choose to default on the loan once the business is completed.

Therefore, the lender must ensure that the borrower has enough "skin in the game," and borrowers will only be able to borrow as much as their independent wealth allows them to.

The lender will only lend as much as they are sure can be repaid.

Will the loan amount lessen the poverty of the Indian entrepreneur?

Why or why not?

A theory or model asks whether something (e.g., microcredit) affects something else (e.g., business profitability, health, or education). Economists often call the "things" in question variables, that is to say, the *things that vary* in the story. There are two kinds of variables. We usually differentiate between endogenous, or "inside," variables, whose levels we want the model to explain (i.e., business profitability, health, and education), and exogenous, or "outside," variables, whose levels we want to acknowledge but *not* explain (i.e., microcredit). Why is this? Because we recognize that the system we are interested in (i.e., the entrepreneur and the lender) is embedded in larger structures that we know are outside of either person's control.

How would a microcredit program be embedded in larger structures? For example, a microcredit program may raise funds from an international sponsoring foundation, or it may be affected by corruption. These are broad factors whose outcomes we can't afford to leave to chance when we think about how microcredit affects poverty—even if the entrepreneur may never be aware of them.

For now, we need some assumptions on how the variables relate. Does microcredit generally lead to less poverty, or does more microcredit result in more poverty by burdening already-stressed entrepreneurs? The *assumptions* we proceed with inevitably shape the *predictions* we end up with.

What assumptions build our story?

ASSUMPTIONS

We might *assume* that the man in India prefers more money to less money. We might also assume that his future poverty (in terms of health and education) depends strictly on whether or not he receives this loan. The prediction then is that the microcredit would lessen his poverty in terms of health and education.

However, *these assumptions don't need to be literally true.* Truthfulness or realism would seem to be a particularly costly thing for a model to give up. So, why don't assumptions of a model need to be literal? *If a model were literal, it would cease to be a model.* But doesn't that mean that a model should strive to be as realistic as possible? Yes and no. Yes, because this would help the theory to explain as much of the real world as possible. No, because, at some point, realism becomes a reason not to tell *any* story, doesn't it? If a story had to include the details of every meal the man from India had or what his favorite color was, it might never get told. This is not to say that a model is free to abandon all sense of realism, only that it is not always practical to include *all* realism, or even as much realism as the audience may like. With that said, the model builder is responsible for convincing the audience that his or her model is appropriate to the situation they are trying to understand. This is important because of the real-life consequences at stake.

However, there is one very important caveat. The assumptions cannot ever contradict one another. The model builder is not allowed to contradict himself or herself. He or she must keep the narrative consistent.

MAKING PREDICTIONS

To understand why predictions are important for modeling, let us add a simple layer to our story. Suppose that the poor Indian entrepreneur we are studying lives in West Bengal and that we are also interested in his diet (see Atkin 2013), as we want to learn more about his health after he receives the microcredit. We want to make an informed prediction or hypothesis about how he would behave upon receiving the microcredit. Let us make two assumptions.

Assumption 1: *This poor entrepreneur prefers rice, which he had more of as a child.*

Assumption 2: *The poor entrepreneur spends more on rice than on other foods.*

Prediction Question: Does how much the entrepreneur spend on rice today depend on how expensive rice was in the past?

It may appear as though the entrepreneur especially likes rice and may not care how expensive rice has been in the past. If he doesn't care about the cost of rice, then microcredit could allow him to buy more of it (than if he did care).

However, let us look at the assumptions more closely. A helpful clue as to which is correct is in the first assumption, which says that the entrepreneur *had more rice as a child*. Why would this be? Perhaps because rice was readily available at that time. Why would this be? Could it simply be because rice was *cheaper* while the entrepreneur was growing up? If that was the case, the amount the entrepreneur now spends on rice would depend on how expensive rice was in the past, at least to some extent, because *the fact that he had more rice as a child implies that it was cheaper back then.* For this reason, the entrepreneur may not necessarily start buying a whole lot more rice just because he is granted microcredit. How much he is comfortable buying would still depend on how expensive rice was in the past.

Again, the assumptions in the story may not be literally true—however, the economist must ensure, to the best of his or her ability, that they do not contradict one another.

We can define the *system* (nearly) however we want, and we can *assume* (nearly) whatever we want, as long as our model is consistent and logical and based on the environment our story is creating and being created in. Defining a system so ambitiously, however, raises a question as old as contemporary development economics: Are the poor similar to or different from most people?

ARE THE GLOBAL POOR SIMILAR OR DIFFERENT?

Coming up with solutions to global poverty through knowledge creation is at the core of many research efforts worldwide. Oftentimes, when someone wants to understand economic theories in the context of global poverty, what they are really asking themselves or others is whether people who are poor are fundamentally different from everyone else or not.

Deep down, in terms of their wishes, desires, and hopes, is the poor man begging on the street in Freetown, Sierra Leone, similar to an Indian entrepreneur needing credit? To what degree does a way of life or culture make a group of people incomparable to others? A person's answer to this is hard to divorce from his or her personal worldview.

This question has endured since the pioneering work of agricultural economist Theodore Schultz, who shared a Nobel Prize with Sir Arthur Lewis for essentially starting contemporary development economics. Schultz joined the University of Chicago in the early 1940s, after the college administration in his previous institution, following political pressure, stifled a report recommending substituting oleomargarine for butter. Schultz's ([1964] 1976) seminal paper famously argued that farmers in poorer countries maximized their returns on their limited resources and environments. Since that work, economists have generally thought that differences between the poor and non-poor were not very important, that the poor tended to behave in ways that were pretty much similar to everyone else. This often eludes other social science perspectives.

Notwithstanding, economic imperfections (such as the ones present in credit markets) actually exemplify broader notions of imperfections in economic systems. The work of Nobel Prize winner Amartya Sen has defined much of this thinking. For example, economics often relies on the ability of markets to support individual freedoms. This important efficiency construct is often based on "Pareto" efficiency (after economist Vilfredo Pareto). Pareto efficiency is any allocation arrangement where it is not possible to make at least one person better-off without making at least one person worse-off. Sen's paradox, however, shows that *no* social system can commit to a minimal amount of freedom, support Pareto efficiency, *and* function in a society (Sen 1970). He also showed that even how we think about who is poor and who isn't can affect the kinds of democratic policies we consider to be the best actions to take in fighting poverty (Sen 1999).

The question of whether the poor are like everyone else or not remains unanswered. Generations ago, many members of the economics profession held the belief that people—whether poor or middle-class—were interchangeable, and they may have been looking for theoretical and empirical ways to use the *similarities* between people as a platform for policy. Today, most economists disagree with this assertion, and they are now looking to understand how *differences* can serve the same end. Whether one thinks the poor are like everyone else or not might speak to a person's perspective on a common humanity and even to whether he or she believes that such a thing exists. It also tells the degree to which we think a common *story* does, should, or can drive human activity in general. Whether we realize it or not, whatever story we favor yields answers to questions. Such imperfect answers (based on imperfect economies) nearly inevitably lead to an imperfect story of development.

The sheer ambition of attempting to tell such a story influences international aid to poorer countries in the policy world. Like aid, our sense of solidarity in research, for better or worse, tells as much about ourselves as it does the people we identify with. Obviously, this implies that economic theories must be, themselves, a certain kind of aid. More broadly, a story tells us as much about the storyteller as it does the story.

But in the end, a common story is all that an economic theory really is.

WHY POVERTY STORIES?

Why do we accumulate all of these models in all the areas relevant to poverty? Do they work? Anyone who has seen the Oscar-winning 1994 film *Forrest Gump* may remember the following dialog:

> That day, for no particular reason, I decided to go for a little run. So I ran to the end of the road. And when I got there, I thought maybe I'd run to the end of town. And when I got there, I thought maybe I'd just run across Greenbow County. And I figured, since I run this far, maybe I'd just run across the great state of Alabama. And that's what I did. I ran clear across Alabama. For no particular reason I just kept on going.

Since I have gone this far, I might as well modify my model using one more piece of information. Whether the model has "worked" and one should stop running poses a dilemma for economists that requires yet another question.

TESTING A THEORY WITH ANOTHER STORY

Can microcredit stop poverty?

How do we get an answer to our dilemma? A theory is tested with data—using a method (another story)—to understand how valid the original story is.

In development economics, theories are often tested with experiments or studies resembling experiments. The most commonly used framework in development is a randomized control trial, or RCT. RCTs in program evaluation are inspired by analogies to medicine, particularly when a new drug is being tested.

In the context of the India microcredit example discussed earlier in the chapter, the logic of an RCT works as follows:

Stage 1: Give a group of randomly chosen entrepreneurs microcredit, and select another group of randomly chosen entrepreneurs to whom you don't give any credit.

Stage 2: Next, compare the outcomes of those entrepreneurs who did receive credit with those who did not receive credit.

If the study finds that those who received the credit are less poor, then it can be concluded that microcredit does reduce poverty in India. If those who got credit are not less poor, then it can be concluded that microcredit does not reduce poverty.

Why is it important that the entrepreneurs be chosen randomly? Suppose we conducted the selection process in some non-random way, such as only giving credit to entrepreneurs who could not read or write. If these entrepreneurs were then slightly less poor following the microcredit, we would be presented with a dilemma: did the entrepreneurs' poverty lessen because of the microcredit or because of something that had to do with their illiteracy? We would be unable to tell.

The same problem would occur if we simply chose people by location. Suppose that we selected entrepreneurs in a certain village to receive microcredit and found a positive effect. Were the entrepreneurs better-off because of the microcredit or because there was something unique about that particular village that we were not aware of? Again, it would be impossible to fully tell.

Randomization has the advantage of sidestepping these issues. By randomizing who received the microcredit, we know that it couldn't have been any other factor *other than the microcredit* that had whatever impact we see (or don't see), precisely because the microcredit was provided at random. A study by Abhijit Banerjee, Esther Duflo, Rachel Glennerster, and Cynthia Kinnan (2015) found that business investments and spending in India increased following a microfinance program, but there were no changes in education, health, or women's empowerment. In other words, microcredit affected how profitable businesses were, but it did not affect the social factors that were not directly tied to an entrepreneur's business.

The change in how microcredit is perceived today may have occurred simply because microcredit programs (which were previously considered successful) had some unique element to them, one that did not generalize, say, to Indian entrepreneurs. A theoretical story tells us what we may expect, and an experiment (or another story) tells us what we found.

However, randomization has its limits in helping us understand global poverty. For example, if we have found that microcredit allows entrepreneurs' businesses to become more profitable, how long lasting would such effects be? The effect of a policy might or might not last as long as we would like. Some studies attempt to track people for longer periods of time to better understand how long poverty action lasts in the life of the poor.

For example, one major dilemma for policy makers around the world is how to encourage more children to attend school. This is important for the ability of education to change the trajectory of children and open up entire worlds via learning. Yet many children in African countries are unable to consistently attend school, for a variety of reasons. School uniforms are often expensive, and what's more, many children must work for their parents—some of whom are in such desperate financial straits that the promises teachers make that schooling can really change a child's life seem too long-term for comfort.

Historically, another major barrier to school attendance has been worm-based diseases. One study by Edward Miguel and Michael Kremer (2003) found that a deworming program led to less absenteeism in Kenyan schools. What would this mean in the longer-term though? The economic argument for child labor instead of schooling is often that the benefits of education might or might not be tangible in the long-term. Well, several years after their initial study, the researchers Miguel and Kremer returned to the same sites with new coauthors and found that the same deworming program they had studied *also* led to the same children (now adults) working more hours every day and participating more in agriculture and manufacturing (Baird, Hicks, Kremer, and Miguel 2011).

Experimentation is increasingly common in the economics of development and has remade the field. Abhijit Banerjee and Esther Duflo (2011) give an excellent overview of experimentation as a middle ground between entirely market-based and large-scale development policy. I visited Ghana in the summer of 2014 to find my former coworkers designing several randomized control trials, and I have made plans to help run some of them. The appeal for many policymakers, I believe, is that experiments take much of the guesswork out of policymaking.

One surprising dilemma experimentation yields for economics has to do with the justification of economic theory itself. Should development be about evaluating a *theory* or evaluating a *program?* As is the case with all dilemmas, not everyone will agree. The dichotomy may be a false one, as a theory, at its core, is only a hypothesis telling us why some policy might affect poverty. But by explicitly incorporating economic theory into program design, we may better understand *why* the poor may behave the way they do. Without a theory, experimentation becomes a "black box" that just tells us what effect a policy had. With the aid of theory, we can update our prior knowledge with the help of experiments and descriptive evidence (Glennerster and Takavarasha 2013). This issue arises because research must demonstrate a causal argument as well as an argument that travels to new contexts. For instance, in addition to knowing that credit improved business profitability in India in our original example, we might be interested in whether the study could tell us anything about *other* markets. Theories can shed light on this, if only to some extent.

In his book *Public Policy in an Uncertain World: Analysis and Decisions,* Charles Manski (2013) provides an important critique of the chorus "the research has *shown*" and an argument to incorporate uncertainty and embrace partial knowledge. Manski shows how strong assumptions often lead to less credible findings than weaker ones. He uses the term "incredible certitude" to criticize an overconfidence in findings, given that some uncertainty must remain beyond the scope of statistical and econometric tools. Researchers are as unpredictable as the people they decide to study. Ad hoc data analysis choices (i.e., subjective choices made for the sake of a specific study at a specific point in time) may impose an element of uncertainty on most results that is hard to unpack. Can *any* result be fully trusted? To protect the integrity of findings, some economists are now advocating that researchers use time-stamped preanalysis plans to state all research analysis plans up front, *before* obtaining any data, and they will then be held to their commitments when testing a theory. (Casey, Glennerster, and Miguel [2012] and Miguel et al. [2014] discuss this need for transparency in economics and quantitative social science research at length.)

An equally urgent dilemma may be how to think about the global poor when the way they behave has little to nothing in common with what our theories assume or predict. Experimental research on global poverty is bringing about a reimagining of what the role of economic theory is and should be. Such work is helping us understand what questions should be asked to better know global poverty.

BEHAVIORAL ECONOMIC NARRATIVES

There are two main issues in the economics of global poverty that are affecting the narratives that help economists know poverty. One issue is that we are no longer certain about how much a poor person is really *homo oeconomicus*—that is to say, an economic construct. Poor people often may not behave in a way that implies that they rigidly follow derived assumptions and predictions, no matter how logical these may seem. This finding, rooted in psychology, is commonly attributed to Daniel Kahneman and Amos Tversky (1979), and it helped create the new field of behavioral economics, which mixes economics with psychology to understand real-life choices rather than decisions that would logically be expected or optimal.

In the above vein, economists are thinking about poverty models even more broadly. For instance, Marianne Bertrand, Dean Karlan, Sendhil

Mullainathan, Eldar Shafir, and Jonathan Zinman (2004) found that, as important as interest rates may be for an Indian entrepreneur, the choice to take a loan depends *just as much* on the person *whose picture happens to be on the offer letter.* Even the most creative person would have had a challenge predicting that! Another intriguing result that may have been difficult to foresee was that, in schools, teachers taught better when students were motivated with a reward—but not when the teachers *themselves* were rewarded (Kremer 2001).

What do these seemingly erratic results mean for theory? In a collection arranged to openly discuss the implications of experiments, Banerjee (2005) noted the need to step out of theoretical comfort zones when thinking about poverty research and policy. How these difficult-to-predict scenarios can make sense in a theory or story—and how much of the standard rational approach can coexist with behavioral theories—is one of the fastest-growing areas in economics. For example, Ronald Harstad and Reinhard Selten (2013) led a forum on whether psychological insights can coexist with standard rational theories, and Xavier Gabaix (2014) ambitiously reimagined much of an entire microeconomic theory textbook with psychological insights.

Notwithstanding such efforts, there is still no unified economics and psychology theory that has gained the reach of the assumption-optimization program. Experiments, in the end, are questions about *how* the poor may become like everyone else, not whether they are like everyone else. However, it is worth remembering that none of the above questions can be answered without knowing who is (and is not) poor in the first place.

POVERTY MEASUREMENT

A common international poverty line was popularized by seminal work by Martin Ravallion (1994) and the observation that many poor nations' self-reported poverty lines clustered around a dollar a day (often adjusted to around $1.25 per day). The poverty line is one of the most powerful and influential concepts in development economics because of its intuitiveness and helpfulness. It may be the most widely used empirical model in all of development thinking.

Usually, poverty lines are defined as simple cutoff points that are determined in relation to an aggregate income or consumption measure at the individual or household level, used to distinguish the poor from everyone else. Multiple lines may be used to represent monetary or even non-monetary terms (such as literacy). A relative poverty line is defined relative to income and consumption in the country of interest, whereas an absolute poverty line is based on a basic standard of what is required to meet basic needs or to sustain a healthy average family. Since poorer countries often have many living on the bare minimum, developing countries tend to use absolute poverty lines, whereas wealthier countries use relative lines.

In an article written for the Center for Global Development, Lant Pritchett (2013) compares poverty lines with reference points that are more familiar. For example, there are constant temperature thresholds at which water freezes and boils and human bodies experience fevers. Somehow, however, existing measurements of poverty lines are nowhere near as reliable. As Martin Ravallion admitted in an online comment to Pritchett's piece, the economic poverty line construct is currently unable to predict such changes in living standards, as far as real-time global poverty is concerned—despite the fact that it has been used to help conceptualize global poverty as a problem. As a model, this was never its intended purpose, as both scholars are aware.

If both scholars are right that a poverty line is not as rigid as, say, a freezing point, the question becomes: *How can we identify distinct differences in living standards among the global poor?*

Debates on how low or high we should set a poverty line transcend abstraction to define the lives of real people. In 2014, for example, the government of India slightly revised its poverty line, which resulted in about 30 percent of Indians (around 94 million) being considered poor, up from the 2011–2012 statistics of 22 percent (Zhong 2014). Although the authorities should be lauded for their initiative, did these "nouveau poor" actually become poorer a millisecond after the change? How do we count the poor if we cannot agree who *is* poor? Angus Deaton (2013) argues that poverty measurement is a manifestation of democratic consensus rather than scientific evidence and warns against an overreliance on such data. To measure poverty, policymakers, researchers, experts, and institutions wrestle with the dilemma of economic measurement and create a united *narrative* of what poverty must mean at a point in time.

Even more distressing dilemmas emerge for the poor themselves, who are rarely a part of such discussions. For the poor, the more interesting issue is whether their identified status would be *followed through* with economic policy. Otherwise, the act of measurement becomes a story without an end.

Why is this important? To the degree that a poverty line is inadequate for capturing subjective experiences of global poverty, poverty *fluctuations* may have little to do with movements above and below the global standard $1.25 line. The poverty line is still a very useful theory for thinking about poverty as a policy problem. We could compare it to when a person turns eighteen years old; there is not always a fundamental shift in an individual's life at that point, but the age certainly remains a useful social and legal barometer.

The problem of global poverty is therefore not merely a question of lower global poverty as a statistical phenomenon. It is rather a problem of how the apparatus of economic theory and experiments can help us know global poverty as an experience. Simply put, it is a problem of knowing and narrating poverty that drives economics and not the other way around. This knowledge most often lies beyond economics, as many economists are aware. For example, according to Karla Hoff and Joseph Stiglitz (2010, 141):

> Psychologists, sociologists and anthropologists have emphasized that the cognitive frames within which people view the world are both collectively held and malleable over time. Category systems have cultural roots and influence what attributes people perceive (Eric Margolis and Stephen Laurence 1999). The cognitive frames operative in a culture unconsciously influence, as well, how people interpret whatever information they register (Marianne Bertrand, Dolly Chugh and Sendhil Mullainathan 2005). Yet economists have generally neglected the role played by socially constructed cognitive frames.

To broadly paraphrase, our interpretation of new information is scientifically compromised, and we are constantly navigating a near-infinite number of dilemmas, all of which are relevant to poverty—often in ways we simply aren't conscious of. The tools humanity constructs to navigate dilemmas are *technologies,* although the role of technology in poverty and development is itself an ongoing dilemma.

POVERTY, TECHNOLOGY, AND DEVELOPMENT

Global stories of technology's impacts on global poverty can be found as far back as the Industrial Revolution. Technological innovations have been a key lever in improving living standards all over the world—with the glaring exception of poorer countries. The rise of mobile telephony in developing countries has motivated many policymakers to attempt to use accessible mobile phones as a platform for service delivery in a wide number of sectors, such as health, education, agriculture, and finance. The degree to which new technologies allow countries to "leapfrog" in development trajectories is exciting, and this is redefining global poverty itself.

In my Poverty, Technology and Development seminar—a new addition to the Global Poverty and Practice Program—students often debated this very topic. The participatory seminar represented an opportunity to transcend different fields and imagine conversations using nothing but scholarship.

A theme that resonated with many was the narrative that Africa is poor due to low levels of science and technology. Much effort in economics has focused on this issue. To explain poverty today using a technology lens, Diego Comin, William Easterly, and Erick Gong (2010) assembled a large dataset of ancient technologies that were important in 1000 AD (such as writing and the wheel) and then expanded the dataset to the year 1500 AD, compiling relevant technologies of that time (such as ships, guns, and printing). Interestingly, the authors found a very strong relationship between technology access five hundred years ago and poverty today. Countries that had access to new technologies five centuries ago were wealthier today, whereas countries that didn't have such innovations in the past were poorer. As William Easterly (2010) put it:

> Britain had all 24 of our sample technologies in 1500. The Democratic Republic of the Congo, Papua New Guinea, and Tonga had none of them. But technology also travels. North America, Australia, and New Zealand had among the world's most backward technology in 1500; today, they are among the wealthiest regions on Earth, reflecting the principle that it's the people who matter, not the places. As migration has transformed parts of the world that were nearly empty in the Middle Ages, technology has migrated with them.
>
> And these differences had already appeared in 1000 B.C.: Late Bronze Age culture in what is now Western Europe already had pack animals, ceramics, and metalwork, while the Central African Neolithic culture did not. In short, the winners keep winning.
>
> As Billie Holiday sang, "Them that's got shall get / Them that's not shall lose."

Paul Lovejoy, a prominent scholar of African history, has a different view. Lovejoy believes that we can't understand science and technology (or the lack thereof) in Africa by looking at Africa per se. In research done for the United Nations Educational and Scientific Organization's Slave Route Project, Lovejoy (2014) argues that we gain a better understanding of Africa's contributions to science and technology by looking at the *Americas* eight years before 1500 AD. Why should we look at the Americas in 1492? One reason is that in the wake of the severe destruction in the Americas following the European conquests and violent land confiscations around 1492, none of the plantation crops and very few foods brought to the newly discovered continents actually came from Western Europe. Instead, most of the crops that were introduced to the Americas came from Africa or were originally grown there. Sugarcane was first grown in Morocco, cotton was cultivated in Sudan for centuries before the slavery project, and rice was grown in West Africa before being introduced to Georgia, the Mississippi Valley, and northeastern Brazil.

Knowledge was not only transferred as is but was also subject to further experimentation. Although historians call this technology transfer the Colombian exchange, Lovejoy argues that this categorization minimizes African agency and the continent's indigenous knowledge of botany and zoology that would eventually inform the modern sciences. In the commercial arena, Lovejoy points out that products such as palm oil–based soap, Coca-Cola, and Worcestershire sauce would eventually benefit from African ingredients.

Lovejoy's argument only seems bound to the past if we assume that slavery does not exist in the modern world. Yet unfortunately, it does—although it takes different forms than it did in the past. According to the FBI, sex trafficking is the most common kind of slavery today, affecting millions of poor people throughout the world, including people living in developed countries (see, e.g., Walker-Rodriguez and Hill 2010). If Lovejoy and the United Nations believe we can understand aspects of current African poverty by following old slavery routes, then (by analogy) we may be able to better understand modern sex trafficking by turning our gaze on the perpetrators as we attempt to understand the realities of the victims. Therefore, a grasp of poverty theories in *history* is relevant for understanding poverty in the present and future. Although we cannot undo the past, history, technology, and development present powerful lessons and urgent dilemmas about poverty today—and even in the future. For example, if technology five hundred years ago had consequences for poverty today, how might technology in 2015 affect poverty in the year 2055?

This provocative question shows how important the voices of the poor might be to technological change. In a study of how technology can empower poor people, my research surveys Ghanaians on their cellphones to understand their preferences for antipoverty policies (Opoku-Agyemang 2015). Randomized voice-based surveys in local languages quantified citizens' perspectives and raised awareness on poverty issues in the news. Some poor people were emotional when they were able to connect with poverty debates for the first time. Sadly, this slight progress excluded people without phones, those who are arguably the *most* marginalized.

During my Poverty, Technology and Development seminar, my students navigated their own poverty dilemmas as they wondered how technology could redefine antipoverty agency among the poor. An illustrative topic for many of them was the origin of the global rubber industry in the Democratic Republic of the Congo, narrated in Adam Hothschild's 2006 classic, *King Leopold's Ghost*. Many Congolese were exploited and killed so that rubber for tires and automobiles—world-changing technologies— could be developed. Such structural conflicts are not confined to the distant past, however. Congo produces most of the minerals found in every computer, camera, and mobile product, not to mention several aerospace and medical devices, and these industries have direct links to recent instability in the country. Shannon Raj (2011), a law scholar at the University of Southern California, calls these "blood electronics." Like most of her peers, Heidi Larsen had never heard of blood electronics.

Heidi was one of my students. She is Danish, of Thai descent, a conversational first-generation sociologist passionate about activism. Interestingly, she told me that she didn't have a social media account— unusual for someone taking a technology-related class. Heidi struggled with experimental intuition and disliked economics, so I joked that Denmark and the United States were probably more different from each other than sociology and economics were. Having made one brave but temporary visit to the field of economics, could she attempt another? She attended office hours, worked hard, and improved. Later, she mentioned her fears that technology would overtake her adoptive father's factory job.

I was surprised at how Heidi reacted to the material we discussed in class. While several students were understandably struggling to reconcile their passion for technology projects with their desire to help poor people in Congo, Heidi suddenly announced that she wanted to use her new skill- sets by joining a social media start-up working on global poverty. When I asked what had changed her perspective, she bravely shared personal thought experiments, mingling the material with her interests: "If most global citizens abandoned technology, would poverty cease, worsen, or remain unchanged? What might labor coercion in Congo mean for any *technology-led* protests, from Occupy Wall Street to Ferguson or even in Congo itself?"

Heidi was pushing herself with questions. Like her classmates who had joined start-ups with engineering students, and even like myself, she had no crystal-clear answers, only internalized dilemmas.

Heidi and other students are not alone in needing to make peace with dilemmas. Beyond the particular case of information technologies, uncertainty is definitive in any imagined future of global poverty. Contexts provide useful dilemmas that are often instructive for policymakers. They too must continue to wrestle with uncertainties.

POVERTY DILEMMAS: BIG PICTURES

A historical lens allows us to revisit our dilemma in a big picture sense. Why do we have global poverty? Or, to phrase the title of the Daron Acemoglu and James Robinson (2012) text as a question: *Why do nations fail?*

This question yields more stories and questions both within and beyond economics. The *geography dilemma* would argue that being in the tropics, in and of itself, can cause poverty. In my first year in college, I vividly remember reading a French gentleman named Pierre Gourou, who argued that the reason African countries were poor was that people were lazy and lacked curiosity since it was so *hot.*

Even if such ideas are no longer politically correct, they still persist, albeit less overtly. That poverty may be a consequence of *space* is seen in the policy focus on *tropical* diseases, such as malaria. Although this relationship is partially true, it is harder to tell whether health issues are *consequences* of poverty or *drivers* of poverty, especially because countries that are tropical (say, Malaysia) are significantly less poor and less malaria prone than many African countries. If health affects poverty and poverty affects health, and we find both increased poverty and worse health going South, *how can we tell which is causing which?* The dilemma remains.

Another dilemma is the *culture dilemma*. Can the way of life of a group of people explain poverty? At first glance, this also seems plausible. Yet, as Acemoglu and Robinson observe, Argentina and Uruguay have more people (proportionally) of European descent than North America does, yet they also have more poverty. It may be too simplistic to assume that a culture dilemma is extinct—it persists in talk of new information technology start-ups that are trying to create an *innovation* culture in the United States that will develop countries' desire to create technology parks. So this dilemma, for better or worse, also remains.

Perhaps the most influential dilemma is what Acemoglu and Robinson call the "hypothesis of ignorance"—what I am calling the *ignorance dilemma*. Simply put, if policymakers only knew the right policy to take, poverty would be history. That poverty remains a global phenomenon simply means that policymakers are unaware of what policy is needed. Some work has found that democracies seem to elect highly educated leaders on average (Besley and Reynal-Querol 2011) and that such leaders' countries tend to grow faster than countries with less-educated leaders (Besley, Montalvo, and Reynal-Querol 2013). Such ignorance dilemmas might be factors influencing the common decision of policy makers to study abroad in Western democracies and implement democratic reforms when they return to their home nations.

Ignorance dilemmas motivate economics research. If ignorance is the main reason for global poverty, then poverty knowledge is the remedy. Yet, even when we think we have the correct policy, it is worth remembering that a policymaker may decide *not* to implement the policy for *political* reasons. Furthermore, the poor may not be politically powerful enough to get a certain policymaker re-elected. If this is the case—that poverty is a political problem—then the dilemma becomes *institutional*. In this sense, whether a country's institutions (e.g., its laws, rights, and political systems) empower the poor or are co-opted by an elite explains the degree of poverty in this story.

As important as all of the above concepts and contributions are, it is critical to also note that, even with the best of intentions, the way a scholar relates to study subjects is very similar to the way a narrator relates to his or her characters. All scholars working on global poverty have power of their *own*, which raises new dilemmas.

STORYTELLERS AS EXPERTS

Any dilemma tale teller is necessarily on a pedestal, as he or she necessarily directs a sequence of events as they occur, while conveniently being shielded from them and from any consequences they may have. The character and the audience, on the other hand, grapple with the tale and its implications.

Scholars working on global poverty are inevitably in a position of power, at least relative to the people they study. They create knowledge that has strong influence on the lives of the subjects of their studies. This is probably true even when a study is strictly theoretical. Power emanates from the knowledge of theories and the ability to use this expertise.

Many social and political science scholars argue that expertise is an *inherently* political process. For example, Tania Murray Li (2007) shows how several development projects around the world attempted to divorce poverty from power, betraying the very people the projects intended to serve. If all models are stories and hence inherently at least partially wrong, then the benefits of drawing rigid boundaries around and rationalizing social processes of global poverty in exclusively technical terms comes at a cost that is *political*—even though this act renders such processes into *adaptable stories.* When poverty is reduced to a technical problem to be solved by an expert, development as a process is often intertwined with political costs, as the rights of citizens in poorer countries are often only *assumed* to be important (see Easterly 2013). It is not very surprising that such approaches to solving policy problems may *reproduce* poverty and create policy challenges that may be *worse* than the problems they were intended to solve (Mitchell 2003). Khalid Kadir asks a similar question in one of our #GlobalPOV videos, *Can Experts Solve Poverty?*

The #GlobalPOV Project, *Can Experts Solve Poverty?*
www.youtube.com/watch?v=8jqEj8XUPlk

Why is expertise problematic for knowing poverty? Researchers must realize that our research renders us part and parcel of poverty worlds. We are all *characters in dilemma tales.* We become *actors* (rather than merely detached narrators) when we choose our variables, when we decide where and how to perform our studies, and when we decide who will (and who will not) participate. We have power over poor people that is not "outside" a theory but that defines poverty knowledge itself. Like poverty lines, however, any threshold separating research from reality can only be an intellectual construct created to impose structure. We have power because the poor live in an environment that, for better or worse, we, as researchers, is constantly affected by our most superficial thoughts. Some relevant research by the World Bank (2015) has drawn attention to psychological biases that experts may have about poor people, such as perceived helplessness. While laudable, our studies are not exempt from an Orwellian dilemma of expertise: all dilemma tale characters are equal, but some are more equal than others.

Paradoxically, one may be most conscious of this point when furthest away from poor environments. The Center for the Study of African Economies (CSAE) annually hosts one of the world's best conferences on African development at the University of Oxford. One unique aspect of the event is that many African scholars (based in African universities) are invited and hosted at St. Catherine's College. The conference provides a unique opportunity to engage scholars who not only work *on* a particular country but also are permanently *based in* said country. One observation that is hard to avoid while interacting with scholars and enjoying the proceedings is a seeming divergence of research interests by geography, which CSAE acknowledged.

On the official CSAE blog, Justin Sandefur (2013) compared the topics the invited African scholars worked on with the topics the other scholars attending the conference worked on, finding some interesting patterns. Whereas scholars based in Africa focused more research on jobs and government policies, scholars based outside Africa focused more efforts on topics such as war and natural resources. Outside scholars were much more focused on international aid than scholars based in African countries. When Sandefur extended the data to include papers that had been rejected by CSAE, he found similar trends. Although finding a way to foster truly globalized economics discussions remains a dilemma, participants still provide thoughtful perspectives, irrespective of where they are from or even what economics sub-field they study, which is yet another advantage of having a broadly common story-telling style that most economists worldwide use.

The interesting thing about Sandefur's finding, however, is that certain dilemmas of expertise remain important. For example, do results hold different levels of sway depending on where the researcher is based? The issue of power and expertise arises because, as the economics research of global poverty becomes an increasingly global enterprise, the dilemma of whose voice is telling what story and for what audience becomes blurred. Like dilemma tales, economics research is at least partly influenced by an audience—in this case, of policy decision-makers. Dilemma tale frameworks may extend discussions to the poor, whose perspectives are lacking in the design of such narratives, although how this should work in practice remains uncertain.

CONCLUSION OR DILEMMA?

Much progress has been made in developing theories and using evidence from experiments and related approaches to help expert economists know poverty. A dilemma tale is a useful way of thinking about how economics research is done, what it finds, and what it helps us to know about global poverty. The research process necessarily presents dilemmas for the audience of policymakers—who must use research results in the real world. However, it also imposes dilemmas on the people the work intends to study and even on economics researchers themselves, as they find themselves part and parcel of global poverty.

The opening dilemma tale showed the importance of legal institutions, which call to mind the rights of poor people to tell their stories. As we attempt to negotiate different "dilemmas of everyone" in our ongoing economics research on global poverty, we should share the gratification we get from grappling with uncertainty with our student scholars, who are also engaging this most important topic of our time. This is an exciting time for future policymakers, who must also make their own contribution to the dilemma:

*How can we **know** global poverty?*

We must give students the **TOOLS** to DIG beneath.....

..a broad, general *INTEREST* in **POVERTY ACTION** TO UNCOVER

HISTORICAL NARRATIVES of a particular *place* or a group of **people**

5 Fixing Poverty

Clare Talwalker

This chapter is about why history and anthropology matter for the world's current fixation on ending poverty. Coming to grips with the history and anthropology of a place matters in a range of ways, but it is especially important in the context of this book, given the past and present domination of poverty action by a utilitarian outlook that is ahistorical and overbearingly self-assured. This chapter explores how utilitarianism haunts and limits us, and it asks the question: How can we use history and anthropology to reach beyond utilitarian approaches to poverty and inequality?

While this chapter and this book reflect on what UC Berkeley's Global Poverty and Practice Minor calls "poverty action," much of what we say is more broadly relevant as a reflection on the challenges and possibilities of meaningful action in the world—especially for those who are just coming into their own as young adults. The quest to find meaningful work has become especially perplexing for recent college graduates in today's world because it is complicated by the knowledge that they participate and are complicit in the reproduction of unequal and unjust social systems. As millennials growing up in the aftermath of the UN's Millennial Development Goals and the call to "make poverty history," many students confront troubling questions: What is to be done? What are they to do? What can they do? How can they reconcile their aspirations and the hard work of pursuing their careers—especially in this era of the Great Recession and student debt—with this millennial call to also engage with the world's inequalities? These questions are not only troubling the millennial student in the global North, they are also being faced by the rising middle classes of many countries in the global South today, often within the very same frameworks of paradox and angst brought on by the sharply class-divided societies of the global North.

In light of these urgent questions about what to do—which are always posed in the context of lives so busy that "non-work" time is too easily collapsed into "turn-it-off" leisure time—a call to devote time to history and anthropology seems insufficient. But such a call is a key first step to unraveling and transcending our commitment to this or that instrumental undertaking. Indeed, the poverty action praxis of which my colleague Genevieve Negrón-Gonzales writes in the next chapter depends on this first step.

Many young people arrive at college having already taken up arms for a particular cause. For example, one of my students was concerned with the horrors of child labor, of which she had read many descriptions and accounts. In college, she found an organization to work with in Nigeria. Later, when she signed up to be a student in our Global Poverty and Practice Minor program, she found herself required to pause and dig into the past and to grow her understanding of West African societies. In the context of her literature review assignment, this student spent a semester researching the history of the practice of child labor and of the regional and global debates surrounding it. She discovered, among other things, that her own passionate belief in the ills of child labor had a history that was caught up in the legacy of European colonialism, its importation of "social reforms" alongside Western political liberalism, and the spread of market-based society to places like West Africa. She came to appreciate that the perception of "child labor" as a problem was caught up in the colonial-era reframing of certain practices as social problems, alongside this era's massive refashioning of social relations by wage labor and a global cash crop economy. History and anthropology matter, and learning about them invariably leads us to move from trying to figure out which available cause we think will best fix poverty to understanding a place better, appreciating the history of the emergence of a problem itself, educating ourselves about the different debates in different places around a certain issue, asking more residents of the concerned place more questions, and ultimately exploring why we are drawn to certain questions in the first place (as our personal reasons are embedded in moral, historical, and political ones).

Another student was very committed to countering the poverty perpetuated by unfair trade practices. He found a fair trade organization in Ecuador with which to work. Just like the student mentioned above, he found himself in the Global Poverty and Practice methods course, where we asked him to pause and consider what historical narratives he ought to identify and work through. After a semester spent researching fair trade and Ecuador, he came away with a range of questions: questions about the history of indigenous peoples in South America and their grappling with the modern state; questions about the possibilities and limits of "ethical consumerism" as an approach to alleviating poverty; questions about the growing role of First World NGOs (including ones focused on fair trade) in places like Ecuador; and really difficult questions about how and whether alternative economies and livelihoods can survive in today's world. These are all questions for which precisely that digging into the past and into the postcolonial condition is necessary to understand how the terms of incorporation into the global market have undermined pockets of subsistence or the possibility of fair and equal global material interdependence. As the splits in the fair trade movement itself reveal, the question our student must ask is: Can fair trade replace those unequal global structures with more equal and dignified forms of economic interdependence?

What can it mean for a student to care about poverty as a general and global problem and to seek ways to redress it? Care of this kind—the kind that comes from the embrace of universal problems and generalizable moral positions—is itself a sort of power and privilege (Butt 2002), and it tends to lead people to solutions—utilitarian solutions—that are not attentive to the things that are distinctive about a place and a people. We care much more about motivating college students to learn about the history of a place and to develop an anthropological appreciation of an issue in that place, as this takes them from their embrace of a particular cause (e.g., human trafficking) to a longer and deeper engagement with a particular part of the world and a particular group of people. Such a transition can open up possibilities and future projects that cannot be known ahead of time, including the possibility of grasping how one's own nation's prosperity is intertwined, often in troubling ways, with the languishing of other nations. Without such a move, there is little hope for us to imagine and embrace open-ended, egalitarian approaches to combating inequality.

The #GlobalPOV Project, *Is Privilege Poverty?*
www.youtube.com/watch?v=IRCrvChWDsM

Concerns for history and anthropology, however, are at odds with the dominant school of options for tackling poverty, which are instrumental, technocratic, depoliticized, and individually focused (i.e., neoliberal)—in a word, utilitarian. This chapter posits that learning about particular histories of particular places can change our lives in two main ways: by highlighting the limitations of an overly utilitarian approach to social change and by sowing the seeds for a more political encounter between, say, a First World student volunteer and a Third World poor person. Such an encounter would entail a reckoning of how the histories of the First World and Third World (the long and large-scale history of national apparatuses, armies, trade, institutions of cultural imperialism, and so on) haunt the face-to-face meetings of students and aid beneficiaries today. These histories cannot simply be ignored in favor of pragmatic goal-oriented poverty action; they must be reckoned with on the way to developing a more meaningful poverty action.

Yet, as college-educated millennials take on poverty action work, it is every bit as likely that the dismantling of an overly utilitarian outlook and the cultivating of a new political selfhood will not happen. So, I begin at the very place where our Global Poverty and Practice curriculum begins, with a consideration of the millennial herself. Who is she? What moves a millennial to focus on inequality or poverty? And what options does she or he have for acting accordingly?

THE MILLENNIAL IN THE WORLD

We use the term "millennial" to talk about college students and young professionals in the global North and global South. Though the term consolidates all the members of a generation, any campus in fact brings together a bewildering collection of individual life stories, and any one student's continued journey through college is unique. My own undergraduate journey began when I, a middle-class girl from India, moved from Bombay to Hanover, New Hampshire, in the late 1980s. On my first day of college in the United States, I discovered myself to be a foreigner who spoke English with an accent. During the first week, I learned I was an international student who did not know the characters on Sesame Street or have a specific American shampoo preference. By the end of the fall, I learned I was a person of color, and by the end of my sophomore year, I embraced other identities along with the social movements they indexed: I was a woman in solidarity with all women; a woman of color in solidarity with people of color; a postcolonial subject in solidarity with others like me (Native American friends and friends from Pakistan, French Guyana, South Africa, Kenya, and so on). It was in college in the United States, far away from home, that I found a particular political selfhood and came to feel how my friendships could enable forms of political solidarity.

Certain classes shaped this process. One in particular stands out: a comparative class on decolonization that was co-taught by two historians, one the son of a Holocaust survivor and the other the son of an American missionary to Gujarat, India. With their help, and in conversations with other students, I saw Indian history partially reflected in the histories of other ex-colonies. I grew a sense of outrage about how European colonialism had led to current-day disparities between modern nation-states.

The 1980s also shaped the process. It was the forgotten decade, when gatherings of communists and other leftists, along with women's caucuses and people of color caucuses, left over from the 1960s and 1970s, were still happening. Yet it was also the era of Ronald Reagan and Margaret Thatcher, when common sense shifted to the right of the political spectrum. In the United States and in Western Europe, for many on the left, this era seemed to cement a sense of alienation from government and political process.

As a foreigner in a North American four-year college, my feelings of outrage and solidarity filled me up for the most part and brought me close to other people. Naturally, like any other teacher, what I recall of my own college journey shapes what I bring to my teaching of college students today. It is hard for me to shake off the expectation that my students, like I was at their age, are searching and that they will find their movement and their feelings of solidarity in college. What I've discovered is that in some ways I am right and in some ways I am wrong. I am right in that students today are certainly searching, and I am wrong in that they appear to be seeking and finding different things than I did. I offer a few composites from the incredibly heterogeneous student body I have met at UC Berkeley:

- Jonathan is the first in his family to attend college. His parents emigrated from Vietnam in the 1980s. He grew up in Southern California, and he wants to be a dentist. He is choosing to work with a dental aid organization in Ho Chi Minh City over the summer; he sees this as a way to help him connect with his parents' history, of which he has heard stories throughout his childhood.

- Heather grew up in a middle-class Caucasian family in the California Bay Area that fell on hard times. She recalls her father having to pick up items for dinner at a food bank when she was young. She opts to volunteer with one such food bank during her junior year and will make the experience the basis of her senior anthropology thesis.

- César is Mexican-American and a first-generation college student. He is the son of divorced parents and is struggling to balance school with translating for his mother, who is seriously ill and needs help navigating the U.S. health care system. He recalls filling out Medicaid applications year after year for her when he was a high school student; they were complicated. He is headed to medical school and, en route, will spend some time working in a free health clinic in Nicaragua.

- Marise is a full-paying economics major from Taiwan, the daughter of a banker who wants her to study microfinance. She does this, and returns home confused, no longer so sure that market access and microcredit are a panacea for inequality, but steeped in the controversies and debates that swirl around them.

These backgrounds, choices, and aspirations reveal and shape a whole range of young adult viewpoints on the world today. They are incredibly heterogeneous, yes; but many scholars are helping us conceive of the shared social and political moment against which this heterogeneity can be viewed as assuming a particular style and genre (Adams 2013; Butt 2002; Giroux 2010; Lawson 2012; Roy 2010). We have a neoliberal student subject, they suggest, who is eager to intervene individually and concretely in the world, with the help of the effervescent market, where possible. We have an overburdened student, for whom a short stint of community service is just the break they long for from the rat race for credentials and lucrative careers. We have a student motivated by one or another particular global ethical campaigns, such as anti-trafficking, human rights, or microfinance. To this list of descriptions, I would like to add that we have a utilitarian student, one who is accustomed to a technocratic approach to social change, an approach that is depoliticized and instrumental, whose energies and longings are feeding the growing industry of volunteer opportunities around the world. Indeed, we could say that the world is being remade so as to offer up more and more perfect venues for these volunteers from the global North, where they can be launched into thoroughly useful action to bring someone out of poverty, to redress human rights violations, or to bring modern health care to someone who had none (Talwalker 2012).

It is hard to say which is shaping which: whether student volunteer demands are pushing the aid industry or whether the energies of the aid industry itself are shaping student volunteer desires and aspirations. Certainly, when I was in college in the late 1980s, there were no ads in student newspapers and on TV beckoning young people to apply for an impactful and fulfilling experience helping people in a faraway country. In the intervening decades, NGOs have proliferated all over the world (Fisher 1997; Leve and Karim 2001), and many social movements and informal community groups have opted to take on official NGO status (in the United States, this is the tax status of a 401(3)(b) organization) for the fundraising potential it offers (Incite! 2007). When today's millennial signs up to volunteer, they do so in a context that is rich and overflowing with similar options. As several scholars are now helping us to appreciate, the ubiquity of such organizations is something for us all to take very seriously because these non-state actors are fundamentally shaping young people's views of the world, its problems, and what's to be done about them.

Today's ubiquitous NGO identifies a social figure (e.g., a faraway orphan, a struggling entrepreneur, a shrinking rainforest, or an undercompensated coffee farmer) and harnesses the affect whipped up by this figure for decidedly utilitarian ends: to draw in funds that are directed at concrete interventions designed to effect specific change in verifiable and measurable ways, which must in turn be reported back to vigilant donors. NGO appeals do to the world what commercial advertising does to local reality—they process it through their own sense-making apparatus, colonizing it, repurposing it, and representing it for very deliberate ends. Images of peoples and places are deployed as grist for the "get-it-done" mill of the international NGO. Such appeals and the NGO model itself are so ordinary and daily for the millennial that they are part of her taken-for-granted landscape and shape the lens through which she views the world and her possibilities in it. This is not only a Northern phenomenon. With the thickening of ties between college-educated youth in different countries through such social media and sharing projects like Facebook and Couchsurfing, we can talk about the global reach of mediascapes and ideoscapes (Appadurai 1990) featuring the NGO approach to global action and social change.

Not all NGOs are the same. The NGO arena includes many different sets of agendas, goals, and theories of change. We are not debating that wide range here, however. Rather, we are considering how the arena presents itself today to millennials as a somewhat unified style of options that come along with the volunteer industry aspect of it: as a confident and articulate world that offers real options for travel and engagement. These options, moreover, are available not on the basis of historical know-how about a place and a people but rather on the basis of a familiarity or interest in an issue or sector, or on the basis of technical or medical or accounting and managerial interests or skills. We might ask: As this arena is professionalized and tailored for advertising and volunteer appeals, what becomes of the kinds of frameworks that are engendered by the study of the past, such as the framework that links India to Kenya, Nigeria, and Algeria and compares the history of British colonialism with the earlier settler-colonialism of Native America. It is not that such a framework is no longer available to those who hunt it down, but it is certainly not a prerequisite for involvement in international service and volunteering.

This framework foregrounded a political identity, whereas most of the NGO arena today presents itself to millennials as apolitical. As a result, we have many students undertaking service-delivery work (such as legal, medical, or public health projects), work in schools, community infrastructure building, issue-specific work (such as human rights or environmental justice work), and market-based approaches (such as corporate social responsibility, social business, or projects of ethical consumerism). The very standardization and professionalizing of the volunteer industry makes it harder for young people to imagine and act upon the much more difficult and tenuous work of learning about a place and a people, reflecting on one's relationship to all of this, and exploring ways to engage its community organizing and social movements.

What does it mean for the utilitarian approach to have trumped other approaches to social change, replacing the various and diverse collective struggle against inequalities, and the different solidarities these engendered, with an instrumentalist war on poverty? What is lost and what is gained?

THE UTILITARIAN ENCOUNTER WITH POVERTY

Later identified as a specific school of thought, the original utilitarian framework was first laid out by Jeremy Bentham in Great Britain in the late 1700s and then elaborated upon by the father and son pair, James and John Stuart Mill. John Stuart Mill spent most of his career in India and wrote at length about how and why Indian society needed to be remade along utilitarian lines, which for him were rational and efficient lines. These three politician-scholars emphasized government legislation that would maximize utility and create the greatest good for the greatest number. They were focused on large-scale reforms, on dismantling what they saw as old-fashioned and silly customs and traditional beliefs, and on furthering what they considered to be smart and technical projects aimed at increasing overall productivity and their notion of the social good. Later, Max Weber would describe such projects as the matter-of-fact embrace of a bureaucratic management of society. The first utilitarians celebrated such management, even as they championed and expounded, in contradictory ways, views of liberal freedoms (e.g., individual privacy, freedoms of the press and of religion, and so on).

The utilitarian approach has shaped and influenced modern society in deep, profound ways. We could say that our modern social structures are fundamentally utilitarian—rational, scientific, and effective (Taylor 1979, 71)—and most people expect them to be so. The power of the utilitarian approach is derived in part from the fact that it is perceived as a matter-of-fact and neutral force of good. In the early years of the modern and bureaucratic state, Bentham became a hero because of his obsession over detailed plans for all manner of social reforms in England, which included the establishment of a decennial census of the population; a general register of real property; an improved system of patents; a ministry of health; a system of public account keeping; armament factories designed on new technical principles, to be eventually run by convict labor; prison buildings designed for optimum surveillance of prisoners; a school to teach utilitarianism to the upper middle classes; and other reforms for public education (which at the time was called public instruction) (Polanyi 2001, 126). Bentham also supported notorious workhouses for the "able poor," advocating that the poor be put to work rather than provided with "outdoor relief" (unemployment benefits), regardless of whether this involved separating husbands from wives and parents from their children.

Utilitarian thinking thus dispassionately weighs the costs and benefits of a particular policy, following with "dogmatic simplicity," as Martha Nussbaum (2004, 63) describes it, the principle of the greatest good for the greatest number, conceiving of an ideal society as one that best prompts individuals to behave productively. In so doing, utilitarian thinking displaces other ways of conceiving of people, replacing these other ways with the view of people as instruments for achieving a pragmatic end. As Karl Polanyi suggests in his book *Great Transformation*, utilitarianism took the instrumental principles of the emerging new science of economics (e.g., individual self-interest, value maximization, the drive to accumulation) and applied them to social and political life.

Arguably, versions of such utilitarian thinking permeate the policies of the modern state and define our social structures. Moreover, utilitarian thinking permeates and constrains our views of personhood, social life, and social change. In such thinking—if we put aside the parsing out of the relationship between liberalism and utilitarianism (see, e.g., Riley 1988; Weinstein 2007) and assume their reconciliation for most intents and purposes of our everyday lives—social change can be imagined in no other way than as "small-scale reform in liberal democracies," and not only is there no alternative to such change, but there "*should* be no alternative" (Weeks 2011, 179).

Writing about liberalism in a wonderful essay, political theorist Wendy Brown (2004, 462) asks if liberal human rights are "the most we can hope for" when we think of justice in the world, noting that, by their centrality, these rights "render . . . other political possibilities more faint." Human rights assume a transformation of other forms of justice—and sometimes even their destruction—a process whose pros and cons are not considered within the liberal framework and its utilitarian extensions because human rights assume a robust state apparatus built on the idea of the liberal individual, and they require and assume a particular style and form of governance that, where it is not already in place, entails a cultural revolution (a destruction of the old) to be instituted. Other forms of justice, such as those grounded in locally specific moralities, cosmologies, kinship ties, and other group loyalties, are brushed aside or forgotten in the process (Abu-Lughod 2010; Merry and Stern 2005), as they appear to be the kinds of silly customs of which John Stuart Mill wrote with impatience. Commenting on the widespread taken-for-grantedness of such Fukuyama-style liberal approaches to justice and social change, cultural critic Kathi Weeks (2011, 181) notes "the official anti-utopianism" of the Right. All possibilities are already known in such an anti-utopia, and much of the past is dismissed as simply illiberal. Any new possibilities or different combinations are considered childish or overly idealistic—unrealistic. And how does such anti-utopianism translate into the realm of higher education? Here, too, it makes the teaching of alternatives increasingly difficult, since curricula are rewritten or approached with a view to realistic application in a preconceived world. Critical educationist Henri Giroux (2010, 184) writes that all this reduces education to "bare pedagogy" consisting of "market-driven competitiveness and even militaristic goal-setting."

The millennial of today must either embrace or take a stand against the instrumentalization of everything, from dreams and aspirations to the desire for a meaningful adult life. This is reflected in the way so many young people think about how best to tackle poverty and inequality in society. My colleagues and I see this every year with each cohort of students in our program. I see it every semester, when the students in my global poverty and practice course first tackle the group assignment I give them: to come up with a project that will in some way tackle poverty or inequality in a local Bay Area setting of their choice, at whatever scale (e.g., neighborhood, city, county, school district). This is a difficult task, however, because we ask them to engage the overused and abused concepts of "empowerment" and "participation," but to do so with concern about their overuse and with overt reference to the political theorists and critical development studies scholars who debate them (see, e.g., Duraiappah, Roddy, and Parry 2005; Paley 2001; Freire [1970] 2000; Wright 2010). Thus, we ask them to consider the empowering and participatory potential of their projects more from the perspective of social critics or activist-scholars than as aid workers or development practitioners (see chapter 6). This most recent semester, as in previous semesters, the first round of ideas that the students shared with the class were all of a kind. Let me share a few examples:

- Target a low-income neighborhood in West Oakland; reach out to residents with literature on the importance of physical exercise and healthy foods; devise some measure for evaluating health in the neighborhood before and after this educational outreach. Goal: improve the health of low-income individuals through exercise and diet.

- Visit low-income high schools in Oakland, spreading a positive and youth-friendly message about the full range of safe sexual health practices. Goal: reduce teen pregnancies, risky sexual practices, and negative self-image in low-income communities.

- Establish a presence in a free health clinic and help clients figure out how to navigate Obama Care. Goal: improve health care access for homeless or low-income individuals.

- Collaborate with a high school after-school program to provide college preparation support and career counseling. Goal: offset the class bias of the college track.

- Teach an after-school class on financial literacy at a high school with a large low-income population. Goal: increase financial literary among low-income youth.

Almost without exception, each group came up with a plan that involved identifying a target group and educating them about a particular issue. Invariably, they would derive what they wanted to teach from some fact about poor people that was established in scientific or social-scientific literature, such as the higher rate of teen pregnancies and the higher prevalence of obesity and diabetes in low-income communities or the difficulties the poor have in accessing existing health care plans. Students would then home in on a plan to educate people to help themselves overcome the problem that they had found identified in some expert literature

We could argue that this overwhelming tendency to focus on educating poor people and to ignore poor people's own views of their own problems is a symptom of middle-class paternalism. We could also argue that it is neoliberal, in that it focuses on individuals and personal responsibility and seemingly neglects the larger more long-term causes of inequity and inequality. These are valid and important cautionary points to make. But I want to suggest a related point (a point that is bound up in these other two, as they are perhaps all ultimately determined by the current historical moment): that this tendency to focus on educating poor people is (also) a symptom of the widespread utilitarian approach to people and society. For utilitarianism focuses on individuals, and it does so instrumentally. It approaches both the social and the natural world as something to be rendered useful for each individual as well as for society at large, and it aspires to a scientific social engineering that would reshape individuals so that society, as a whole, can become (by its standards) a better place (Taylor 1979, 69).

Just as it did when it was first developed, the utilitarian approach today gives a privileged role to those thought to know best about what will produce the greatest good for the greatest number—these are usually experts from the comfortable classes of society. In other words, the utilitarian approach today, as in the past, is top-down and paternalistic. We might think it is inevitable that large-scale and complexly interdependent societies will require bureaucratic management, and that is certainly true. But this chapter points out that we cannot note this without also always posing the question: What consequences does this have for society and social relations?

Moreover, as with the first utilitarian reforms, the utilitarian approach today is fundamentally liberal, in that no state program is conceived that

is hostile to (or presents an alternative to) the workings of the marketplace or that directly threatens the principles of individual liberty. Today, this specifically means the utilitarian approach will lead to projects that assume and encourage personal responsibility and an entrepreneurial spirit. Furthermore, it will facilitate as light-handed a role for the state as possible, except in those cases where a state is necessary for the protection or facilitation of market forces themselves. In the eighteenth century, for example, the state imposed customs tariffs that favored national markets and built infrastructure that supported commerce. Similarly, today, we might view the 2010 Affordable Care Act as extending health care not only by extending state-run health care plans but importantly also by mandating and regulating extended private insurance coverage.

These characteristics of utilitarianism heavily inform our students' choice of education projects for their group work. Each group of our students came to the conclusion that poor people's lack of knowledge was the main problem, and therefore the solutions they proposed involved educating poor people. They did not consider or imagine that there may be other ways for relatively affluent adults with higher education credentials to interact with the majority of the world's population—people who are neither affluent nor in possession of any educational degree. Furthermore, reflecting the ahistoricism of so much instrumental aid work today, the students did not think of how the "ignorance" of the poor is itself historically and socially constructed.

It is just such a depiction of the poor as ignorant that provided the fuel for the remaking of society into its modern and liberal form, imagined and instigated by utilitarians. While utilitarians wanted to protect the liberal freedoms of every individual, they took a special interest in poor and working-class individuals. Such individuals, in the utilitarian worldview, needed to be taught a great deal before they could make the best use of liberal freedoms and properly flourish in a free market society. For example, early utilitarians devised Poor Laws (which were not unlike the post-Clinton New Welfare Laws) that discouraged what was viewed as dependency and encouraged individual hard work. They also advocated for prisoners to produce marketable goods, thereby paying for their own imprisonment. Overall, their projects sought to orchestrate the ever-greater productivity of the poor and working classes. In their view, for the social good, an individual could and should be encouraged to produce to their greatest potential. This belief led them to support special projects for poor and working people, who were seen as needing special reshaping or education to be prepared for their participation in the perfectly, rationally, and effectively administered societies of the modern world. Therefore, the education of the poor and the working class person and the cultivation of ordered, liberal societies were together the unique goal of utilitarians.

Though such goals seem self-evident to our contemporary minds, it is crucial to keep in mind that they emerged in a specific context. Historicizing what we take for granted is the only way to begin questioning the universal guise in which such goals otherwise appear to us. It was in Western Europe—specifically in Great Britain—that utilitarianism and liberalism first emerged at a time when Europe's colonization of Africa and Asia enabled its rapid industrialization. It was in the context of the deepening economic interdependency of the world market, which was dominated by European colonial empires, that the liberal state form of Western Europe was able to consolidate. Utilitarian goals and approaches, notwithstanding the specific time and place from which they emerged, appear universally appropriate and relevant to us now. They dominate our minds and the minds of our students, and it is difficult to think beyond and outside them. Yet how can we apply them today and continue to make assumptions about governance and citizen-subjects in the solutions we imagine without noting that the circumstances are different?

In their perception of the poor as ignorant and needing education (to be provided by either private or state actors), our students also embrace a utilitarian ambition. Overwhelmingly this semester, and in previous semesters, my students were at first compelled to imagine what information gap (such as those regarding sexual health or nutritious diets, for example) they should go out and fill in order to help people help themselves. And, though the assignment expressly invited students to think about questions of power, definitions of expert knowledge, and people's own involvement in any social change around them, still they returned with ideas for educating poor people. It did not come first to their minds to consider how different groups had their own forms of knowledge or their own ways of making sense of expert knowledge (Corburn 2005). Their logic was that, since poor people faced barriers to gaining knowledge, they would destroy those barriers by personally taking that knowledge to them, thereby helping poor people get the very same access to health care plans, financial literacy, sexual health knowhow, and so on that the normative middle-class citizen enjoys.

There is a certain matter-of-fact sense to this approach. That is precisely the power of the utilitarian approach—it has come to seem like common sense. Indeed, it has come to seem like the *only* possible common sense. Yet this book raises a concern with this so-called common sense—this view of social change that is based on a scientific social engineering. We ask: What are the alternatives to such a view of social change, and how can young people today learn about, appreciate, and, now and then, come to avail of these alternatives?

In another context, the philosopher Charles Taylor pointed out that our public lives and our structures of government are dominated by the utilitarian approach. He noted that, as this utilitarianism came to monopolize modern Western society, a reaction emerged in the form of Romanticism—a reaction whose sphere of influence, he believed, was limited today to certain social arenas. He wrote:

> The Romantic strain has been contained, as it were, in modern Western civilization. . . . Modern civilization has . . . seen the proliferation of Romantic views of private life and fulfillment, along with a growing rationalization and bureaucratization of collective structures, and a frankly exploitative stance towards nature. Modern society, we might say, is Romantic in its private and imaginative life and utilitarian or instrumentalist in its public, effective life. What is of ultimate importance in shaping the latter is not what its structures express, but what they get done. (Taylor 1979, 71)

Whereas utilitarianism emphasizes getting things done, Romanticism is oriented toward understanding or intuiting how society—its projects, its buildings, its art and literature, its governing institutions, its corporations, and so on—is or is not expressing the spirit (the imagination or the emotional or symbolic life) of its people. In other words, the Romantics raised questions about how social reality hangs together, how social structures do or do not express the aspirations, dreams, character, and history of a particular community. The Romantics posited that such questions mattered more than the instrumentalist remaking of social life wrought by science and rationality—that, indeed, it mattered especially much given that radical remaking.

Considering this contrast between the Utilitarian and the Romantic prompts a whole series of questions for us: Can we talk of a Romantic approach to poverty action? Should we do so? What are the pitfalls of doing so? If Romanticism opposes utilitarianism, and particularly if it takes issue with the utilitarian focus on increasing the efficiency and productivity of every individual in modern society, then what image of the human being and what vision for human encounters might it offer in its place that we, dreaming and seeking to act for a less unequal world, can explore and consider borrowing? And how might a Romantic approach to poverty action relate to this chapter's call to attend to the history and anthropology of a place and issue?

BEYOND UTILITARIAN APPROACHES TO POVERTY ACTION

Romanticism is often described as a response to the overly rational forms of Enlightenment thought with its reaching for universal laws and rules and its ideas of progress that could and should apply to all human beings everywhere. By contrast, Romanticism pondered the uniqueness of a people and a place and reveled, as did its high priest, Jean-Jacques Rousseau, in the radical freedom of each individual and in the life of the emotions. Some scholars view the Romantic era as historically contained, running from the late eighteenth to the early nineteenth century. Others consider this period to be merely the starting point for ongoing and enduring cultural critique and resistance to overly instrumental or rational approaches to people and daily life, and thus its legacies and its contemporary traces and echoes can be explored today (Casaliggi and March-Russell 2012). For example, Taylor suggests that the current environmental movement's concern for sustainability might be viewed as a return to Romanticism's original focus on humans as a part of nature.

For our purposes, as we wonder how to reach beyond the utilitarian apprehension of people and of inequality, the Romantic critique of utilitarianism offers us inspiration. The Romantic school of thought opposed the atomism and instrumentalism of Enlightenment and liberal, utilitarian philosophy. Where utilitarians are focused on how large-scale projects *work* most efficiently and rationally for every individual, Romantics are focused on how small- and large-scale human endeavors—such as a poem or the mining industry (see Ziolkowsky 1992)—*express* a particular era and a particular people. So, were we to consider drone technology, for example, a utilitarian might be drawn to the fact that drones can be used to deliver medical supplies to remote parts of Burma, whereas a Romantic might contemplate what drone technology expresses about our modern times, such as our desire to extend our bodies and our will across national borders. The utilitarian would be less concerned with interpreting what drone technology says about how humans act today (such paths of thought would likely make a utilitarian impatient and contemptuous) and would instead highlight how drones can be effectively used for the greater good. For the Romantic, however, the practical uses of drone technology are beside the point and shortsighted if the full moral, political, and even spiritual implications of "drone-ness," if you will, have not been thought through or understood.

It is this kind of interest that makes it possible to relate a historical and anthropological imagination to the Romantic critique of utilitarianism. It is that predilection to dig deeper, to strive to understand the meaning and context of things and the story of a people, that led the Romantics to belittle the utilitarian philosophy of stripping matters to their bare bones for instrumental remolding. The Romantics loathed and feared that approach, in which people and things merely served as instruments and raw materials in a large plan. And just as Romanticism was at odds with utilitarianism in the past, today the call to think of history and anthropology is usually met with the impatience of those many poverty actors who are focused on impact and impact evaluation.

The Romantics were interested not so much in how to manipulate nature and society to meet human needs and desires but rather in how a society, in harmony with nature, comes to express the spirit of its people— what the Germans described as the *Volksgeist*—in its institutions and cultural forms. However, there is also a dark underbelly to Romanticism. Historians note that this preoccupation with the spirit of a people can be traced from the writings of philosophers to the rantings of political leaders—in some of whose hands it became aggressive and xenophobic, more about fighting to preserve and protect a particular people's spirit at all costs and less about recognizing other and varied *Volksgeists*. The line from Romanticism to German nationalism to Nazism, then, is that dark underbelly of Romantic thinking. Any quest for alternatives to utilitarianism ought certainly to steer clear of those shoals. And Romanticism has been accused not only of nationalist chauvinism but also of male chauvinism and androcentrism, with feminists noting that Romantic poets, who were mostly male, did not so much consider a female perspective but rather used the figure of the woman in their creative work to express male yearnings (Mellor 1998).

We would not need any such detour through the vast literature on Romanticism itself, however, if all we intended to do was simply borrow something of its impulse—its wariness of utilitarianism's hegemony—to rethink student and lay participation in aid work or poverty action. For, as it turns out, precisely this wariness underpins the writings of those many scholars who are distraught by the current instrumentalist and technocratic approaches of development, service learning, and international volunteering.

Indeed, the Romantic response to utilitarianism appears to me, as an anthropologist, to be analogous to many an anthropologist's response to poverty interventions. Just as Romanticism pushes back against an emphasis on efficiency and order with a concern for human spirit and imagination, anthropology asks how a particular poverty intervention makes sense to a particular group—for example, how a conditional cash-transfer program (an exchange of cash between people and a modern state) bumps up against existing understandings and practices of debt and obligation, social relationships, and the relationship between people and things. Asking what a Romantic alternative to poverty action today would look like and feel like is not unlike asking what an anthropological imagination brings to today's poverty interventions. Romanticism is a school of thought, a set of critiques and questions, a sensibility, whereas anthropology is an entire academic discipline. The two are distinct, but I suggest that they provide similar tools to help us grapple with and critique the utilitarianism of poverty action.

The world's focus on poverty, we believe, needs to foster curiosity among young people about particular places and their histories. We want our students to develop an appreciation of the struggles and victories of these places and what those struggles and victories mean to different groups in them, and of other more mundane things too—these places' music and musicians, their food and languages, their landscapes and railways, their truck routes, their cities and building materials, and more. Such an appreciation is a necessary first step toward understanding the political framework in which ongoing change is happening in these places. Indeed, we care more about fostering that involvement in and curiosity about places—about helping students figure out how to relate to a part of the world (be it the place where one of their parents comes from or a country of their choice) and learn to encounter others in it and act in it—than we do about an individual student or an individual organization taking up the charge of fixing that place's poverty.

This chapter stresses the crucial importance of all types of scholarship that push back against the taken-for-granted liberal and utilitarian consensus on poverty and inequality action. If not necessarily Romantic as such, this scholarship is important for its historicizing of liberalism and its openness to multiple frameworks of understanding. Consider, for example, the alternative economics and alternative politics of J. K. Gibson-Graham and Erik Olin Wright. In their realistic reckoning with the current global political economy and their imagining of ways to not simply reproduce inequality, their work is inspiring. Both writers are pushing for new ways to think and act toward political and economic futures, futures that are less unequal and in which people enjoy better collective control of their lives because they are less subjected to market forces. Both write to steer us beyond the current impasse on the left. They borrow from, but also depart from, Marxist views on overturning capitalism, arguing instead for "hybrid" systems: small- and large-scale experiments that coexist with the nation-state and the market. Such positioning makes their appeal extend, potentially, far beyond merely those on the left. Indeed, they write for wider audiences. Yet their writings bring into question the widely held assumption that extending liberal market society is the panacea for all social problems. For our purposes here, we might also read them as departing from that overly utilitarian planning that frames people as individual producers and consumers, and society and nature as the mere raw material in grand plans for a version of improvement that puts the marketplace center stage. Their writing encourages and allows for a much richer (i.e., a fuller and more overflowing and open-ended) vision for people and for humanity. For in their writing, we find the seeds and the tools for reimagining and remaking our social lives and for cultivating "an experimental, performative, and ethical orientation to the world" (Gibson-Graham 2008, 613). Moreover, especially in the case of Gibson-Graham, the writing of these two scholars is infused with the Rousseau-style Romantic faith in the essential goodness of human nature to be compassionate and the recognition that harm (i.e., the unequal treatment and the unequal conditions of life) comes from faulty modern institutions that we can transform, in small and big ways, through steadfast experimentation and through celebration of others' experimenting.

Gibson-Graham and Wright put center stage experiments that are actually unfolding around the world—ranging from local cooperatives and local consumption decisions to a city-level budget planning experiment to the global and virtual Wikipedia experiment. In detailing such examples, Gibson-Graham and Wright demonstrate that their writing is more than a professional scholarly enterprise; rather, it is a political program that makes visible where and how other peoples' creativity and experimentation are actually improving lives. In Wrights' (2010) terms, such "real utopias" are providing people better livelihoods and control over resources (economic power), letting people make the rules by which they live (political power), and allowing people to work together and influence others (social power). For Wright, in other words, to evaluate if something counts as a real utopia, one must ask if it is enhancing economic, social, and/or political power for the people involved. Gibson-Graham and their collaborators talk of "diverse economies" and "community economies," and they emphasize that, while no one experiment is perfect, the very fact that there are people actually experimenting all over the world is cause to stop and notice, and cause to celebrate. They write:

> We foreground people who are negotiating the challenges of living well together. . . . They want to make a difference. The decisions they make and the actions they take may not always be to our liking; we may think the trade-offs involved are insufficient for the task at hand. But these are our fellow travelers. . . . Like hundreds of thousands across the globe, these are the people who can teach us by opening up new worlds of possibility. (Gibson-Graham, Cameron, and Healy 2013, 15)

Other people, in this fresh and inspiring view, are less individuals to be acted upon living in societies to be modernized and improved, and more people with histories doing what they can to survive and live well. These scholars do not only attend to this individual scale, however; the place and role of institutions and modern states is also key to their theorizing. Indeed, to counter the dominant utilitarian thinking of young adults today, we might invite them to consider "real utopias," such as those offered by Gibson-Graham and Wright. If we can all do this, we have some hope of escaping our predilections for fixing the problems of others and for thinking that the utilitarian approach is the best and only approach possible.

FROM A UTILITARIAN APPROACH
TO A POLITICAL ENCOUNTER

My students' first drafts of anti-inequality projects were decidedly utilitarian. All focused on educating poor people (e.g., about the importance of
exercise, sexual health knowledge, or signing up for medical insurance
through the new government health act) so they can help themselves. Those
projects were transformed through the course of the semester as the students mulled over readings that dealt with power, place, and history. Several
groups were unwilling to abandon their focus on education, but all of those
groups switched their projects to educating children in schools rather than
educating adults in their communities or work places. The most popular
projects turned out to be those that involved educating high school students
about health and nutrition, including sexual health (although this may have
been a reflection of the high numbers of public health and pre-med majors
in this particular cohort). "Ideally," wrote one group in their final report, "we
will create a comfortable environment to learn about and engage with these
topics, thereby allowing the students to make informed, safe, sexual decisions through our provision of knowledge and resources. STDs, unplanned
pregnancies, abuse, etc. can all hinder young people's ability to reach their
full potential, and [our organization] will help them avoid and cope with
these issues to the best of our ability." Another group targeted the after-
school hours as key trouble hours for low-income and unsupervised high
school students and proposed providing a space for them to socialize and to
receive career counseling and healthy snacks.

Yet four other education-focused projects deserve special mention for
how they fused pedagogy with visions for social change. Of these, two
came up with plans for elementary school children. Both focused on
immigrant groups and on helping integrate the first languages and home
cultures of immigrant children into the school environment while simultaneously educating the rest of the schools' population about the different
immigrant backgrounds of these students. "[Our organization]," one of
the groups' report explained, "[targets] children ages 10–11 who are in the
5th grade because of the moment of transition they are going through in
their lives." The group proposed facilitating open discussions with the
rest of the school about the experience of being an immigrant, including

talking about the experiences of students who were legally documented and those who were undocumented. The hope was that these conversations would "spark the interest of civic engagement" of all present.

The other two projects, also through the structure of after-school classes, focused pointedly on facilitating student-led projects for change. One proposed a weekly after-school art class for fifth-grade students that would be run by college volunteers in coordination with teachers from the school. During the class, students would "create a final project focused on arts funding in public schools." The other project envisioned college students teaching high school students "about the industrial food system," with the goal that, at "the end of the year, students will present at a community event with local leaders to advocate for healthier and locally-based [*sic*] school lunches." Though focused on education, all four of these projects reached beyond a passive learning model to something far more radical.

Three groups focused on state welfare—health care and transportation—and imagined ways it might better serve low-income populations. The two groups with projects involving health care proposed ways to help people navigate the health care system, one of them at the basic form-filling stage and the other providing more long-term assistance by cultivating a "partner" to serve individual people who struggled to access and maintain their own health care. This latter group wrote: "[Our organization] provides [homeless and low-income individuals] a 'partner' throughout the whole process of care, from navigating the healthcare system and available resources, to making the trip to the clinic or hospital with the client, and to following-up with him/her as to ensure that he/she is satisfied and is responding well to the care they have received." The group focused on transportation devised a plan to support the transportation needs of low-income people that would function similar to food stamps. The final group proposed facilitating conversations between different groups in a city—high school students, community leaders, local NGOs, local businesses, city council members, and homeless individuals—and would then use the information from these discussions to plan a social media campaign.

Every student strove for better ways to imagine people's participation and shaping of these projects. In each case, this meant backing away from a programmatic approach and a concrete goal and instead opening up to the unpredictability of what other people think and do. While it was thrilling to watch this shift occur in a written assignment in our class-room, what would it take to bring such a shift to one's engagement with poverty action—or action against inequality—in the world?

In practice, of course, making this shift is a far greater challenge. It can be unsettling to aspire to engage the world without concrete goals, as this requires us to open ourselves up to the unpredictability and unknowability of the other (Kapoor 2004; Spivak 1990). I would like to tell the story of Vaibhav Birla, an Indian-American student who traveled to a midsize city in South India with an organization focused on disseminating information about the importance of handwashing (for countering diarrhea and other infectious diseases) to people living in an informal settlement. When he returned, he described his discomfort with the mismatch between the organization's goals and the perspective he felt he gleaned of the settlement residents. They were not convinced that handwashing was the solution they most urgently needed for the various problems they faced. And Vaibhav himself felt awkward teach-ing people how to wash their hands, as though they didn't know full well how to do so. In his case, educating poor people for their own good turned out to feel awkward and insulting. He also reported that there were problems with marketing hand sanitizer along with teaching handwashing, as the residents of the settlement were not thrilled with its fragrance.

Vaibhav felt he had an advantage over his fellow overseas volunteers because he had a minimal grasp of Hindi, and this helped with rudimen-tary conversation in the settlement, which was home to migrants from other parts of the country. He described talking as much as he could to as many people as were willing to talk with him. He even conducted a focus group during his time in the settlement. As he later told us, it was in this focus group that he picked up that what people believed they most wanted and needed was a local person who could serve them as a community health worker, someone close by who could advise them immediately when they fell ill or were worried about their health. Vaibhav dwelled on this feedback, and in time he decided that it was a thing worth working on with the community. The task came to fully occupy his mind. He returned to the town in India the next summer and discovered that a local hospital had a training program for community health workers. With the help of the residents, he identified a local candidate interested in becoming a health worker for the settlement and put her in touch with the hospital.

This is a story of a student who let himself abandon a concrete goal (teaching handwashing and sanitizer use to a specified number of local residents and devising a way to measure impact) because it felt misguided, and instead opened himself to the unpredictability of what other people think and do. It helped that he had some facility in the language the people he was working with spoke. We could also describe him—due to the fact that his parents had been born in India and that he had taken prior trips to India—as having at least *some* feeling for the history of the people he met in India. Cultivating a feeling for the history of a people and a place—a feeling that, in the absence of a parental link, can be gained by digging through library shelves and reading novels, for example—makes it less possible to act on these people as upon objects in an experiment. Indeed, we might say that growing a historical sense of a place and an understanding of its society is a key tool for dismantling utilitarian thinking.

However, understanding and gaining an appreciation for history and anthropology is not simply a matter of amassing historical facts and memorizing lists of cultural traits and beliefs (Brown 2008; Davis 2010). When my students declare, "I never liked history," or, "History is not my thing," as I sometimes overhear them doing, I feel sure that what they dislike is having to reproduce facts for a grade. When I talk of a historical and anthropological sensibility, I am referring more to a *feeling* for the past and for how it shapes the present, as well as the ways it affects us, others, and our encounters with others. An equal encounter—an "ethico-political" encounter (Kapoor 2004)—with another person rests on some reckoning we do of our shared and varied pasts. Among other things, these are the pasts of our respective nations and their past relations of exchanges—of wars and goods and people and ideas. Accounting for the past and cultivating a feeling for how we are shaped by histories allows us to make sense of the world's poverty and inequality with attention to power, which is what historian Michael Katz (2015) and many others have advocated we must do. When and where such accounting permits a feeling of solidarity—what Massey (2007) has called "interplace solidarity"—are the moments in which we have the possibility of an ethico-political encounter, one that is, we should note, not utilitarian. It was just such a series of encounters, I believe, that Vaibhav must have had with the people living in the midsize city in South India in which he found himself teaching handwashing and distributing hand sanitizer bottles.

CONCLUSION

The impulse and expectation is that volunteers and aid organizations approach their work thinking concretely and instrumentally about what they will do. They thus imagine they will teach a certain number of young women financial literacy, explain to a certain number of families what counts as more nutritious food and what it takes to ensure better oral health, or motivate a certain number of school children to aspire for higher education and better jobs. Of this instrumental approach, this chapter asks a series of questions, including: Who decides what will work best? What views of people and social relations informs such a project? Is the organization a neutral tool of change? Or is it too a phenomenon with its own social framework, viewed in specific and varied ways, informed by long histories of interactions between nations, by the people who it seeks to benefit?

We also note that such instrumentalism is itself derived from a long history of utilitarian thinking about society and about social change. Such thinking, with its singular focus on measuring the utility of everything, is impoverished. It is, in turn, tied up with the rise to prominence of the poverty framework itself. We seem to lose more than we gain when we embrace that framework. What all of us need, as many scholars and activists have pointed out, is to pose questions about inequality in the world. "Inequality" implicates all of us in its evoking of power and political economy and the interlinked histories of nations, whereas "poverty" suggests a bounded problem requiring outside intervention.

The word "politics," however, has become something like a cuss word for young people today. It is not that they are apathetic—millennials are fed up with that accusation, and of being constantly compared to their peers in the 1960s, '70s, and '80s. Rather, their energy is increasingly directed toward pragmatic, measurable action, action whose impact can be appreciated in the dominant language of economics. "Politics," for them, is that dirty business that attention-seekers dabble in; it is that time suck one must do everything to avoid. Yet, in this chapter, we have argued for a shift from thinking about utilitarian solutions to the world's problems to thinking about history and ethico-political encounters and, perhaps, projects for change that emerge from such thinking.

6 Teaching Poverty

Genevieve Negrón-Gonzales

The University is a critical institution or it is nothing.

Stuart Hall (quoted in Giroux 2013)

THE CONTRADICTORY LOCATION OF THE NEOLIBERAL UNIVERSITY (STUDENT)

Growing up in the 1980s, I remember the lengthy Save the Children ads that would crop up unexpectedly in the middle of my Saturday morning cartoons. The ads, slow and set to somber music, featuring an older, white celebrity past his or her prime, featured pictures of children who lived "a world away." Anyone could "adopt" one of these children for "less than a penny a day" and in exchange get a little picture and a letter to carry around as proof of the good they were doing. I grew up in a Mexican Catholic family a few miles away from the U.S.-Mexico border. This faith tradition, mapped onto this specific geographic location at this particular moment in time, coalesced into a pro-poor, Latino Catholicism that would serve to be the foundation of my entry into progressive political activism a few years later. The children in the Save the Children ads looked like me, like my cousins, like the kids on my block. Despite my early exposure to these pro-poor politics, there was something eerie to me about those ads that ate up my carefully rationed TV time—those white women squatting down next to Black and Brown toddlers, the slightly-too-anguished sound

149

of their celebrity pleas, the pocket-sized pictures that proved their existence, and the call-right-now number flashing at the bottom of the screen—
that made the whole thing feel like an infomercial, although the exact
"product" one could "purchase" was not exactly clear.

The world of poverty action my students are growing up in is very different—much slicker, much smoother, much more glamorous. Who knew
that eradicating poverty could be so chic and effortless? One can purchase
overpriced scarlet lipstick from the VIVA GLAM line at the M.A.C. cos-
metics boutique, a shiny red iPod from the Apple store, or crimson Nike
shoe laces that are inscribed with the words "lace up, save lives." These are
all products in the (RED) line, a division of the ONE Campaign, which
epitomizes the sort of poverty action many in the millennial generation
grew up with. That is, many millennials have been raised within the context of this sensibility about poverty action, but it also profoundly shapes
who they are. The ONE Campaign was founded by iconic rock legend
Bono and is explicitly non-partisan. It works to "raise public awareness
and work with political leaders to combat AIDS and preventable diseases,
increase investments in agriculture and nutrition, and demand greater
transparency so governments are accountable to their citizens. . . . ONE
works closely with African activists and policymakers as they fight corruption, promote poverty-fighting priorities, monitor the use of aid, and help
build civil society and economic development" (ONE Campaign 2013).
The ONE Campaign is not about development aid, which it implicitly suggests is an outdated and ineffective way to combat global poverty, but
rather frames itself as an awareness-building initiative that "educate[s]
and lobb[ies] governments to shape policy solutions that save and
improve millions of lives" (ONE Campaign 2013). Its success rests on a
partnership with big-name multinational corporations like Apple, Nike,
and Coca-Cola that serve as a marketing and product-generating arm and
a multiracial cast of celebrities like Chris Rock, Benicio del Toro, and Julia
Roberts who sell not just the products but, perhaps more importantly, the
image.

We do not single out the ONE campaign or its (RED) line as a particularly egregious form of poverty action but rather as the quintessential
example of the kind of poverty action model that has risen to prominence,
shaping the consciousness and sensibilities of a generation of young

people who draw on that foundation to intervene in the world of global poverty. The ONE Campaign is not simply an example of how millennials understand global poverty—which is to say that they have an acute aware-ness of it and also that they understand it within the context of this par-ticular frame—but it is also an example of the ways in which a neoliberal logic is intricately intertwined with this framework, thereby positioning millennials as neoliberal actors within the field of global poverty action. The ONE Campaign draws on an explicitly neoliberal framework to sup-port its efforts to engage a generation of people in "making poverty his-tory." Within this framework, consumption is positioned not as the prob-lem but as the solution. The (RED) website boldly claim: "As consumers we have the power to save millions of lives each year." This statement is particularly contradictory and problematic given that many of the project's contributing companies have well-documented records of abuse and exploitation and can therefore be implicated in the production of poverty in the global South. The union-busting tactics used against Chilean Starbucks employees, the abuse of Foxconn workers assembling the iPhone5 in Shenzhen, China, and the child-labor practices in Nike sweat-shops in Cambodia are only a few examples.

As many scholars have noted, this consumption-oriented approach to alleviating poverty is a hallmark of the current trend in poverty action. What better way to enlist the participation of U.S. consumers in the eradi-cation of global poverty than to not only allow their consumption patterns to go unquestioned but actually recast this consumption as charity. Thus, far from connecting the consumption of luxury goods in the United States to the exploitation of the labor, land, and natural resources of the global South, these young consumers—and there is little doubt that the target audience is young people—are given a way to satisfy both their material desires and their consciences at the same time.

This is the heart of the neoliberal discourse—the assertion that it is the market that is best situated to solve problems of inequality and that more consumption is the means to accomplish that aim. Moreover, the ONE Campaign approach situates the individual as the actor in the process of poverty alleviation, thereby reifying the power of the individual as opposed to identifying the structural reasons that poverty persists. The campaign's commitment to "monitoring aid" that is granted to the global South and its repeated insistence that the campaign is not asking for people's money but rather for their support evokes the neoliberal suspicion of "welfare" or "public aid." This complements its commitment to "fight corruption," which positions the Third World as a backward place led by greedy people who are in need of policing by the West.

Neoliberalism, of course, is not confined to the realm of development or poverty action; neoliberalism is a global, multisector project. We draw on Henry Giroux's (2014, 1) articulation that neoliberalism is a political, economic, and social project that "construes profit-making as the essence of democracy, consuming as the only operable form of citizenship, and an irrational belief in the market to solve all problems and serve as a model for structuring all social relations." In its centering of profit, consumption, and market rule, neoliberalism's reach is vast and deep; it is, as Giroux (2014) argues, the defining logic of our time, implicating all social, political, and economic relations. Neoliberalism has come to be the defining logic of the current political economic moment in the United States, though its roots stretch back many years, and it is an extension of what the people of the global South have been confronting and resisting for the last thirty years. The implementation of structural adjustment policies, cuts to the social safety net, defunding of public goods and services, privatization, marketization, increases in policing, and the use of surveillance and military forces to quell dissent are nothing new. In fact, the neoliberalism we see today is very clearly situated as part of a broader trajectory of imperialism, neocolonialism, and the growth of global capitalism (Harvey 2005). Still, I argue that we are also experiencing a moment of a particular kind of coalescing around a neoliberal logic that, while it is not new, is experiencing a sort of acute rebirth.

Central to this analysis is a conception of neoliberalism as, in Jamie Peck's (2010, xii) words, an "open-ended and contradictory process." In his book *Constructions of Neoliberal Reason*, Peck pushes against the notion of neoliberalism as a totalizing, monolithic system, casting it rather as a necessarily incomplete and inherently contradictory project. This conceptualization of neoliberalism prioritizes its function as a hegemonic project; it is an engagement in the fostering of a politics of participation rather than simply a politics of domination. This is the nature of the neoliberal project—it has created a common sense reality that is difficult to imagine oneself outside of. Raymond William's (1978, 109) articulation of hegemony is instructive in this conceptualization: "It is just in this recognition of the *wholeness* of the process that the concept of 'hegemony' goes beyond 'ideology'. What is decisive is not only the conscious system of ideas and belief but the whole lived social process as practically organized by specific and dominant meanings and values." Understanding neoliberalism as "creeping collectivism," a term from Stuart Hall's (1988) analysis of the Thatcher years, urges us to consider the power of a project that is necessarily engaged in building consensus rather than the exertion of power through the exertion of authority. Hall's charge to interlocutors in this debate, then, is to consider resistance not simply as engaging in a fight against the state but as fighting for the space to build a viable alternative to the state. Ananya Roy's (2012, 274) commentary on Peck's work directly links this conception to the millennials we find in our classes, calling them "the interlocutors of what Peck designates as 'soft neoliberalism,' steeped in ideas of social entrepreneurship, microfinance, self-help, and creative capitalism." Thus, an important aspect of what it means for this generation of young people to grow up within and through this context is to understand that even their responses to neoliberal policies are embedded within this neoliberal logic. This is the power of neoliberalism—it is not a totalizing force that maintains legitimacy through authoritarian rule but rather a insidious force that weaves a consensus that ensnarls us, even, and perhaps principally, when we consider ourselves to be operating outside of it. This entanglement creates the context within which students arrive in our classes. Like the Washington Consensus and Margaret Thatcher's 1980s slogan, "There is no alternative," this moment is being marked by a steadfast allegiance to neoliberalism not only as a global project that shapes the structure of the economy but also as a hegemonic project that shapes the way millennials see the world, the way they understand its problems, and the way they articulate, envision, and imagine solutions to those problems.

One of the places we can most clearly see this coalescing of neoliberalism and its manifestation as an adaptive and constantly reconfigured regulatory project is in the field of higher education. Higher education has, since its inception, been deeply inscribed with questions of power, race, and equity. Both historically and currently, higher education is situated as contentious terrain and is an institution centrally configured in the struggles around the growth of global capitalism, neoliberalism, racial privilege, class antagonisms, and gender disparities and equity.

We have seen an explicit reliance on the idea of profit as the bottom line for universities. Programs, departments, and disciplines are increasingly evaluated based on their market value, their profitability, and their potential return on investment. This is the neoliberalization of higher education—the turning of our institutions of higher education into places where decisions are driven by profit, where students are consumers rather than learners, where professors are expected to deliver a consumable, digestible product rather than create space for critical thinking, and where competition rather than critical thinking are valued above all else.

The neoliberalization of higher education has been well documented in recent years by scholars like Henry Giroux (2014) and Chris Newfield (2008). The positioning of the university as an institution within the market economy and an insistence that it be governed, developed, and evaluated based on the rules of the market is nothing new, though we have seen a resurgence of this trend in recent years (Washburn 2005). The cost of higher education is skyrocketing, pushing many students out of university life and rendering higher education inaccessible to low-income students (Newfield 2008). The rise in college tuition has also resulted in the amassing of a staggering amount of student debt by this college-aged generation (Maisano 2012), debt that often traps students in a cycle of borrowing that culminates in them leaving college early, without a degree in hand and owing thousands of dollars.

Corporate encroachment on university life (Soley 1995) has ushered in a sort of "academic capitalism" (Slaughter and Leslie 1997) that positions the university as a commodity on the market economy. We have seen an increase of corporate contracts in the public university system, and these influence research agendas and research priorities and shape intellectual life on college campuses. We have also seen an attack on the tenure system—put in place to ensure academic freedom and autonomy—which not has only compromised the integrity of the university system as a space for critical thinking and innovation but has also created a labor crisis via a reliance on poorly compensated and insecure adjunct labor (Giroux 2014).

The neoliberalization of higher education means sweeping cuts will be made to programs that impact student achievement and growth. This is particularly significant when considered within the broader context of a neoliberal economic order that positions the university as an institution that will usher in the transformation of the United States into a "low wage nation" (Bousquet 2008), in which employment for people at the bottom rung of the socioeconomic ladder is characterized by insecure, low-wage, temporary work without benefits.

At the same time, however, history shows that universities and university students have always played a critical role in bringing about social change and social movement. From the student demonstrations at the National Autonomous University of Mexico against the 1968 Olympic Games to the civil disobedience across the United States in the 1960s that led to the establishment of Ethnic Studies to the student protests against South African apartheid and the U.S. intervention in Central America in the 1980s, student movements have been a critical site of resistance and served as a catalyst for social change around the globe. Higher education is an incubator for radical ideas, a testing ground for the practice of democracy.

Given this history, critical scholars and students situated within the university context must grapple with the questions: What happens when the university is packaged up, made palatable, marketed, and sold? What happens to the people, to the thinking, and to the dissent? This is what is at stake in this moment of the neoliberalization of higher education. The university system is being Walmarticized. It is being sanitized. It is being stripped of its ability to function as a critical institution. The results of this transformation, then, are not simply higher fees, temporary labor, and fewer resources for marginalized students but a broader project concerned with a rearticulation of the function of higher education in society. We must now seriously consider the question of how this rearticulation has shaped the generation of young people who have grown up within this context and how being located within the space of the neoliberal university positions them in a very particular location, from which they come to the work of poverty action.

Why does this matter, what is at stake, and what does this mean for the education of these students as global poverty actors? Neoliberalism, embodied by initiatives like the ONE Campaign, weaves a particular kind of dialog about poverty: it is inevitable; it can be resolved by individuals like us; the market is a key part of how this resolution can happen; and the solution lies in the integration of marginal and struggling economies into global capitalism. It uniquely positions people in the United States—but only those who care and are willing—to bring about this broad-based, sweeping, monumental reform—to "make poverty history." This narrative renders invisible the reality that poverty is *produced* rather than naturally occurring and that our consumption in the First World is intimately tied to scarcity in the global South. It obscures the existence of poverty right here, "at home," hiding it under narratives that shift the blame onto pathological people with bad habits who make bad decisions. It ignores the people, organizations, and institutions that have been leading the fight against poverty for decades in the global South. By situating poverty as the result of individual pathology, it silences the reality that "making poverty history" requires a fundamental challenging of the institutional arrangements that produce poverty in the first place.

Our students have grown up with a sense of poverty as something far away in the world. They have been sensitized to want to do something about it, yet they lack an institutional or systemic analysis for this work. What we have found in the work we have done with these students— and in what they have taught us as we have cocreated this qualitatively different methodological and pedagogical project that is global poverty studies—is that a unique kind of opportunity has been created by this set of circumstances. These students are passionate, ready, and empathetic, but they lack the analytical basis and the institutional framework to ask the right questions, engage in a truly helpful and thoughtful way, and think in critical ways about what it means for them to be engaging in poverty action. These contradictions do not mean that it is impossible to do this sort of work from the location of the neoliberal university. Rather, they presents us with a particular kind of opportunity, along with a set of ethical questions about what it means to teach our students in this context and prepare them to do this work. They come looking for answers to their questions, concrete directions for their passions, and a resolution to the quandary of global poverty. What they find, however, are not easy answers but rather a process that brings the complexities of global poverty action to the surface, that instructs them to dig into its nuances and uncertainties and to understand its dialectical and necessarily contradictory nature.

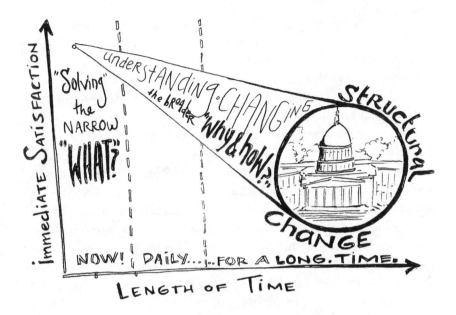

FROM BLUEPRINTS TO A PHILOSOPHY OF PRAXIS

Christine was a sharp, analytical, and compassionate young woman, who I met after she spent four months working with women and children in India as a part of an Indian NGO. As a woman of color who grew up in a lower-middle-class family in the United States, she was personally transformed by the experience, but she was unsettled by the reality that her personal transformation may have been the only real product of her time in India. Disappointed and disillusioned, she struggled with the question of impact; the organization she had travelled to India to work with had seemed to be doing such great work on paper, but the reality on the ground was a different story. She was particularly frustrated because, rather than stumbling blindly into this project, she had spent months researching NGOs—talking to people, weighing options, and comparing various organizations. She saw herself as a part of the generation of young people who could make a meaningful impact on global poverty, and she thought of her future as intertwined with poverty action. She came to me ready to commit her life to making an impact, although she just did not know how to do so. In a moment of exasperation, she told me, "I am ready to do what needs to be done. I just want to do good work. Just tell me which organization, in what place, is doing good work, and I'll go!"

Students come to poverty action because they are called to it. Some are called to it because they personally have experienced injustice, poverty, or inequality. Some are called to it because they are coming to terms with, and attempting to take responsibility for, their privilege. Others are called to it because of some sort of humanitarian principle, political commitment, religious conviction, or "do-gooding" sensibility. Regardless of how and why students are drawn to this work, they all want to figure out the *right* way to act. They want to know what the best program is—the one that is achieving some sort of measurable success while avoiding making mistakes or falling into the neocolonial traps or the "White Savior Industrial Complex" (Cole 2012). They want to know that their time and energy are being spent helping to solve the world's problems, not making them worse. Christine's exasperated statement summed it up perfectly—this generation of young poverty actors do not want to be bogged down by assessments and false starts; they want to pour their love and energy and dedication into something that will *work*.

A fundamental part of the educative process for these eager young people, so full of heart and ready to give, is to teach them that this action-based orientation is part of the problem. There is no such thing as perfect poverty intervention, not because nobody has gotten it right yet but because "perfect," "poverty," and "intervention" are all complex fields of power that are marked by an ever-changing context that cannot be captured through universal metrics, statistical analyses, or detailed spreadsheets. Furthermore, the "find-me-the-perfect-program" approach assumes a sort of neocolonial, teleological process for poverty alleviation that situates poverty as a "problem" in need of "fixing." Moreover, the rush these students are in to identify the perfect poverty intervention points to their impulsive nature—they are compelled to *act* as a way of coming to terms with the reality of global poverty.

Certainly, this is what we want. We must be invested in helping incubate and support this generation of young people who care deeply about the world around them and consider their lives to be intertwined with the struggle for social change. At the same time, we know that enthusiasm can be dangerous and good intentions can be deadly. While we are invested in bringing up the next generation of young people ready to act in the field of poverty action, we must be thoughtful about bringing them up in a way that is grounded in an analytics of wealth and inequality and rooted in a historical context cognizant of dynamics of power and privilege. What students think they need is a blueprint for how to solve the poverty "problem"; what they really need is a philosophy of praxis. And it is precisely this that is the power of the pedagogical process of global poverty studies—its refusal to bring clarity to the complex questions that the eradication of global poverty poses.

On the Space between Theory and Action

A colleague and I were talking recently about a student she had that was putting up a lot of resistance in class, largely because the theory she was using and the conceptual frameworks she was teaching collided with his understanding of the world. In this particular case, this student was unwilling to accept the idea that opportunities and privilege—not merit alone—shape college access. In his view, he was enrolled at one of the top universities in the nation because his hard work and dedication had allowed him to gain entry, and he was unwilling to acknowledge the role that his educational, race, and class privilege had played. My colleague was frustrated that he was so resistant, and she lamented that the thing that makes teaching beautiful is also the thing that makes it difficult: the reality that the teaching and learning encounter is one small moment in a much larger trajectory for our students. At times, this reality fills us with hope—for example, when a former student is engaged in meaningful work in the world and reflects that her experience in our classrooms was a defining moment in placing her on that path. At other times, this reality is less rosy—such as when a student does not get quite as far as you would like him to in class, but you must nonetheless send him back out into the world hoping that some combination of life experience and future (formal and informal) education will allow him to travel the rest of the distance you had hoped to cover. The point here, though, is that these are two sides of the same coin—the "teaching moment" can only lay a framework from which we can hope the student will act, but the true learning comes when the student goes into the world to put this framework into action. This is a story about the space between theory and action.

Students understand this—it makes sense. Literacy theory may make sense while sitting in a classroom of other future educators, for example, but it is an entirely different thing to put that theory into action with a group of five-year-olds. Similarly, a nutritional supplement designed in a lab to counter child malnutrition is only as good as it proves to be in the trial run on the ground. Students in the Global Poverty and Practice Minor are intimately aware of this slippage between theory and action, and for that reason, they are often anxious to go out in the world and do poverty action. They are often skeptical of theory because they consider it a counterweight to "action," which they regard as what actually brings about change. However, what we have seen over and over again is that engaging in poverty action is only one small part of the developmental process of our students becoming actors in the world, acting on global poverty. It is here that we turn to praxis, because praxis not only makes space for this process and understands it by accounting for the cyclical nature of learning, it requires it.

There is a common folk story I grew up hearing about a small village located at the base of a long, winding river. One day, the villagers are out enjoying the sunshine, when all of a sudden they see a baby floating down the river. The baby is struggling and gasping and about to drown. The villagers rush to the river and fish the baby out. Everyone assumes it is just a single, crazy occurrence, but then they turn around and there are two more babies coming down the river—struggling, gasping, and about to drown. Naturally, the villagers also rush to fish them out of the water. As soon as they rescue them, they see three more babies coming down the river. The story continues predictably from there—as soon as they fish out these three babies, four more come down the river, followed by five more. Pretty soon, the entire village is engaged in the rescue effort. It's a frantic mission—as soon as they fish out the babies, more come down the river. All of the members of the village line the embankment of the river, working to save each and every baby that comes downstream. The situation escalates, getting more untenable by the moment, and it requires every single one of the villagers. Soon, one villager steps back. The other villagers shout at her: "What are you doing? We need your help! Without you, these babies will die!" The villager replies, "I am going upstream to stop whoever is throwing all these babies into the river!"

This is a story I often use with my students to illustrate the myriad complexities embedded in social change efforts. It is about the complex interplay between structural change and temporary solutions; about daring to go against the grain when everyone else is going along with it; and about asking hard questions and making hard decisions when there is no clear course of action. But it is also about the interconnectedness of action and reflection. Before we get to the part of the story about the villager who steps away from the line, we are with the villagers. We are compelled by their actions—they make sense to us. The villagers are doing what we imagine we would do if we found ourselves in this scenario. We sense their franticness, and we understand it—it is the only course of action that makes sense. Yet, when one of the villagers speaks up, we see another path, and we begin to question what we hadn't questioned before. We understand how, though the compulsion to act is logical, action alone can trap us in a repetitive cycle that itself might be contributing to the problem we are acting upon. In this sense, the story is also about the important unity of action and reflection.

What Is Praxis?

The term "praxis" is used in various traditions and disciplinary contexts. Marxism has been called the "philosophy of praxis," a description that most scholars believe is tied to an assertion Karl Marx (1978, 143) made in *Theses on Feuerbach:* "Philosophers have only interpreted the world in various ways; the point is to change it." Beyond economic theory, praxis is considered a methodological underpinning in a variety of professional fields, including social work and experiential education. It is also frequently used in the nonprofit sector. Though there is a commonality in the ways in which the term is used in these various settings (it is often synonymously interchanged with the notion of "thoughtful action"), our analysis explicitly draws on a conception of praxis that is articulated in the work of Brazilian popular educator and philosopher, Paolo Freire.

Freire pioneered popular education through a program of literacy pedagogy aimed at the illiterate poor in Brazil in the second half of the twentieth century. Freire's literacy programs are regarded as models within the field of popular education because they represent an educational practice that connects the development of concrete educational skills (literacy, in this case) with political action. At the time, literacy was a requirement for voting in Brazilian elections, so these literacy programs were therefore also political interventions. To Freire, literacy was not just about the ability to read text but also about the ability to read the world. He considered literacy to be "a vehicle by which the oppressed are equipped with the necessary tools to reappropriate their history, culture, and language practices" (Freire and Macedo 1987, 157).

One of the foundational principles of popular education is a disruption of what Freire called the "banking model" of education, in which the teacher, who is positioned as the possessor of knowledge in the educational relationship, makes a deposit into the empty (and therefore deficient) student. In contrast to this conception of the uneducated or illiterate as deficient and in need of outside intervention, popular education builds upon the experiences and the analyses of marginalized people in the educational encounter. Popular education is fundamentally about providing space for the poor to reflect on and analyze their own lives and social conditions and, in doing so, to develop the skills, in community with others, to change these oppressive conditions.

Freire ([1970] 2000, 34) asserted that education is never neutral: "Education either functions as an instrument which is used to facilitate integration of the younger generation into the logic of the present system and bring about conformity or it becomes the practice of freedom, the means by which men and women deal critically and creatively with reality and discover how to participate in the transformation of their world." Freire's work and writings have inspired generations of activists, students, and thinkers to disrupt traditional educational models and practices and develop models based in the idea that the marginalized and oppressed possess the knowledge they need to change their own circumstances and build a more just society.

Praxis is a central component to this pedagogical and methodological approach. Freire ([1970] 2000, 33) defined praxis as "reflection and action upon the world in order to transform it." There are three interventions embedded in this definition that deserve further exploration. Firstly, Freire's conception of praxis is, at its heart, an insistence that education must be action oriented. Praxis posits that learning is not simply about individual fulfillment or deepening knowledge but rather about transformation, not only of the self but also of the world around us. Freire argued that learning without action is empty, that we learn in order to act in the world around us, and that learning (and therefore also teaching) must be explicitly oriented toward that aim. It is not enough for people to come together in dialogue for them to successfully gain knowledge of their social reality. Secondly, learning should not inspire *any* kind of action but should specifically catalyze *informed* action. In his insistence that learning must be tied to action, Freire also argued that this action must be grounded, informed, thoughtful, careful, not simply action for the sake of action. Lastly, praxis is about the unity between action and reflection. Learning, to Freire, is about a forward-moving continuum that is defined by a loop of action-reflection-action; action and reflection must be inextricably connected to one another if we are to move forward. In short, praxis is a pedagogical and methodological approach that relies on the unity of action and reflection to transform the world around us. It is this sort of forward-thinking reflective model that is critical to the educational process of young people coming to terms with their role in global poverty action from within the (physical and intellectual space) of the neoliberal university. This builds on Freire's ([1970] 2000, 43) assertion that, "looking at the past must only be a means of understanding more clearly what and who they are so that they can more wisely build the future."

What Makes a Praxis Orientation Unique in Poverty Action?

A praxis-oriented approach may seem obvious. But as instructors working with university students who lie at all points along the spectrums of class, race, and gender privilege, we see the need for a praxis-oriented approach daily. We use praxis as a method that helps students take responsibility for looking not only backward and forward but also simultaneously inward and outward. The "outward" orientation requires that students think beyond themselves, that at every step along their path of "action" they consider the broader context, the significance of the action, and the ways in which the action is a part of a global constellation of interventions. As Cynthia Rosenberger (2000) argues in her critique of traditional service-learning models, "We need to create a service-learning experience that extends beyond 'empathy' and 'helping others.' Important as these are, service learning must be an avenue of education that enlarges students' critical consciousness and contributes to the transformation of society." It is a way of coming to terms with one's own insignificance and a way of thinking about what needs to be done.

Yet a praxis-oriented approach also mandates that we look inward. It requires that students think about who they are and how they come to poverty action work—not in a navel-gazing way that situates poverty action as an act of benevolence but rather in a way that requires an honest engagement with questions of positionality, power, and privilege that so often fall out of the conversation in the name of taking action. This is partially about recognizing the ways in which power and privilege are embedded in social location, similar to the "invisible knapsack" Peggy McIntosh (1990) speaks of; this process is often the first time privileged students are asked to consider the ways in which they materially benefit from these privileges. It is also about building a kind of analytical and personal recognition that requires students see the ways in which privilege and oppression are co-constructed and mutually dependent.

But an insistence on praxis-informed work is not just about changing the way students think, it is about changing the way that they engage in informed action. "Praxis" is not shorthand for reflection; it is reflection with the specific intent to move forward, shaping future action. In the world of poverty action, there is no shortage of quick fixes, technological innovations designed by experts, opportunities to help the "less fortunate" by giving them something you no longer want, and consumption-based interventions that provide shoppers with the opportunity to help eradicate poverty with the purchase of a lipstick or a dollar tacked onto their grocery bill. At a moment in which taking action to alleviate the suffering of those in poverty is steeped in market-oriented production and consumption strategies, it is important for us to complicate the "just act" message imparted to young people. What we need is not simply for the members of this millennial generation to go out and do something—*anything*—but for them to think critically about what taking action means. That is praxis. It is a methodological commitment to not simply act but to do so intentionally, to not simply think but to do so in a way that inspires action. If it seems like navigating a delicate teeter-totter in which tipping too far to either side will land you in the danger zone, that's because it is. Without an explicit intent to take responsibility for constellations of power and privilege, students can end up inadvertently reproducing the dynamics of colonialism and oppression, which is disrespectful to the work that is happening on the ground in marginalized communities, and ultimately doing more harm than good. As Sara Grusky (2000) reminds us, "Without thoughtful preparation . . . and critical analysis and reflection, the programs can easily become small theaters that recreate historical, cultural misunderstandings, and simplistic stereotypes and replay, on a more intimate scale, the huge disparities in income and opportunity that characterize North-South relations today." Our approach to preparing students to be global poverty actors, then, must be embedded in an acknowledgement of the power and privilege one brings to the table, a sense of the power-laden field one is engaging in, and also an orientation that mandates a continual jumping of scales to consider how interventions have the power to create but also the power to destroy. What praxis does, then, is dig into that contradiction rather than obscure it, and it positions *this* as the work of poverty action, not the act of going elsewhere and "giving back." Significantly, praxis *is* the work of poverty action—not the additional work or the optional work or the auxiliary work but the central task of those who are positioned in this fight.

It is critical that we root the particular poverty-intervention work students are doing within a broader analytical context about how the poverty "problem" came to be, how the intervention arose, and how others think about it, engage with it, and understand both the problem and the solution. Drawing from the field of engaged scholarship, it is critical that students understand that they are not being deployed in this field of poverty action to help but rather to learn. We expect them to contribute meaningfully to the work of organizations and initiatives, although it would be dishonest and disingenuous to imagine that our students are some sort of gift to the people they are working with, for, and alongside. This is not to say the students do not do good work or meaningfully contribute but is rather an acknowledgement that, even with the best intentions and the most rigorous preparation, the dynamics embedded in the service-learning or community-engagement model are unequal power dynamics that, while it is responsible to make every effort to mitigate, will never truly fade away. It is therefore irresponsible to not be honest about this, and true learning can emerge from this space of acknowledgement.

The central idea, then, is that a praxis-orientated pedagogy and methodology are imperative in guiding student learning and student action. Praxis, as derived from these particular historical and theoretical lineages, takes for granted that the compulsion to act that we see in these hopeful, enthusiastic students is not generally accompanied by the compulsion to reflect. Our mandate as their teachers, then, is to foster this reflection and to create this compulsion. Our students must deeply and intimately understand that praxis is a critical component of poverty action because without it, the work we do is not accountable to the communities we work with. A praxis-oriented pedagogy challenges the notion that is often implicitly and explicitly interwoven into the student-centered dialogue around poverty action and poverty interventions—that "acting on poverty" can be a transformative experience for the *self*. A praxis-oriented pedagogy and methodology reminds us—not once, but over and over again—that, though individual transformation may be a desirable byproduct, our central concern is the transformation of *society*.

PARADOXES AND PRAXIS

In this section, building on the key importance of a praxis-based pedagogy and methodology, we would like to take up the question of paradox and praxis. As we have been arguing in this chapter, a praxis-based methodology allows us to reveal the paradoxes endemic in global poverty work, repoliticize that which has been rendered "naturally occurring," and resituate the work of global poverty action not as "intervention" but as reflection-based, thoughtful work. It is important that we identify the paradoxes that are at the heart of global poverty action and remind ourselves that, in the pedagogical encounter, the purpose of poverty action is not to resolve these contradictions but rather to identify the enormous potential embedded in the space that they occupy.

Naturally, our students' desire to smooth out the contradictions and "find the answer"—that they do not take the existence of global poverty at face value and that they want to forge a new way forward, even if there is no clear path to take—is important in that it is part of what drives them in the first place. Their search for answers often makes them want to resolve these contradictions. Our pedagogy, however, requires students to sit with these contradictions rather than regarding them as problems that need to be resolved. In the work we have done educating several cohorts of students in the Global Poverty and Practice program, we have seen several key paradoxes arise in this process. What follows in this section is a brief discussion of three of these paradoxes. This is not an exhaustive list, but it is a way to begin a conversation about what it means to navigate what are at times conflicting and contradictory poles.

American Exceptionalism

American exceptionalism is alive and well in the discourse and practice of poverty action, and it is important for students to understand the ways in which, by positioning themselves as actors in the poverty action world, they inherit a legacy of neocolonialism and imperialism. On a broad level, this requires them to grapple with how not to reproduce these sorts of dynamics and acknowledge that it is particularly difficult not to do so when the ground has already been tilled for that reproduction. On a personal level, students must get engaged in a substantive conversation (and reflection) about where the United States is located within the international financial arrangement and develop an understanding that their access to particular luxury items that allow them to be engaged in poverty action (e.g., cell phones, laptops, and a warm bed to sleep in at night) are not outside of the context they are working to disrupt. This is necessarily a conversation about history, about situating current conditions within long legacies of colonialism, imperialism, and the development of capitalism. It is about helping students understand that their lives look the way that they do because of the international mutual dependency between the global South and the global North. Our students are not simply lucky or blessed to have access to what they have access to, they are the winners in a global financial arrangement because of their birthplaces, and it is critical they understand that the suffering of others is directly connected to that prize.

This is also important in thinking within our national context. I recall a computer science student who was passionate about getting computers into poorly funded California schools. However, she had not even considered the possibility that these schools might have more pressing needs (like functioning toilets). Our students deeply, profoundly benefit from the international arrangement that they seek to change. Students often want to believe in a kind of social change that alters the dynamics of global poverty to raise everyone's standard of living to that of middle-class U.S. residents. One of the key paradoxes of helping train students to do poverty work is requiring them come to terms with the fact that consumptive practices they participate in *cause* global poverty. Consumption in the First World is made possible by the exploitation of the global poor living in both the Third World and in the First World. Students often approach these ideas from a "rights" framework and implicitly or explicitly uphold the belief that all people should have the "right" to live more like us. We seek to build an understanding that it should also be the "right" of the global poor to stop us from living the way that we do. This creates a tension, and it is a struggle that requires a real grappling with the questions of consumption, luxury goods, and our inherent complicity in these exploitative dynamics by virtue of living in a capitalist superpower, even if we choose to engage in transformative work from this location.

Grappling with Critique and Making Peace with Uncertainty

There are times when a teacher knows that the real teaching will only happen when she discards her agenda for the day and instead focuses on what is in the classroom. The week the KONY 2012 campaign went viral, I knew I had an obligation to discuss it with my students rather than stick to my carefully planned syllabus. This decision opened the door to one of the richest conversations that I ever facilitated as a professor in the Global Poverty and Practice program at UC Berkeley, despite the fact (or rather because of the fact) that students left with more questions than they came in with.

KONY 2012, a social media campaign launched by the U.S.-based organization Save The Children, called for the arrest of Joseph Kony, leader of the Lord's Resistance Army, a Ugandan guerrilla group. The campaign, which was controversial from the start (see Cole 2012 and Leonard 2015), raised questions about the ethical dimensions of a U.S.-based organization led by white Americans calling for military intervention in Africa as a means to bring about what they considered to be justice. My classroom was split between students who were sympathetic to the campaign, although critical of some aspects of its strategy and messaging, and students who regarded the campaign as the latest manifestation of the White Savior Industrial Complex (Cole 2012). We had an open-ended discussion that hit most of the important points I had hastily scribbled down while watching the campaign's video myself for the first time at midnight before the class. We talked about how the director, Jason Russell, had juxtaposed images of his own innocent white son against those of the dark-skinned Joseph Kony; about the implicit call for U.S. military intervention as a "peace" tactic; about the way the video positioned a white kid in the United States as knowing what is best for the African people; about the reality that Joseph Kony was not a new threat and was likely no longer even in Uganda, thereby undermining the premise of Russell's proposed intervention; and about the idea that a long-standing, complex domestic issue in Uganda could be somehow resolved by kids in the United States wearing wristbands and wheat-pasting posters on their walls.

What was most instructive about the conversation, though, was what happened towards the end of it, when one of the students turned to me and said, "So, what's the answer? Is KONY 2012 doing more harm than good or the other way around?" It wasn't simply that the students were positioning me as an authority figure in the classroom—they really wanted the right answer. I suggested that the questions, complexities, nuances, and contradictions that had been brought up in our discussion were, in fact, more about the work that each of them was engaged in than about the KONY 2012 campaign. Even if we resolved the questions about this particular campaign, I told them, the questions would remain—not in abstract, but in their own work.

One of the things that can be the most challenging about the preparation of enthusiastic students who want to change the world is helping them develop a grounded approach to critique. On the one hand, we want students to think in a nuanced and skeptical way about any "fix" they encounter to a problem as large and complex as global poverty. On the other hand, it is an easy cop-out to argue that no interventions or initiatives are perfect, so we might as well do nothing. Here, again, we must consider the ways in which the neoliberal university produces particular kinds of political subjectivities. Students who are concerned about the alleviation of global poverty are often going against the neoliberal grain. With a degree from UC Berkeley, most of these students have the opportunity to pursue professions that would easily secure them a spot in the upper middle class. In fact, many UC Berkeley graduates do just that. Thus, a key paradox in preparing our students is equipping them with the skills to be able to critique and analyze poverty interventions (like the ONE Campaign) while simultaneously helping them avoid criticizing themselves into a corner where no intervention anywhere is ever perfect, thereby justifying apathy or inaction. Our students are trying to forge a new way—considering what it could mean to be a truly socially responsible physician, for instance, an engineer rooted in the pursuit of initiatives that can change the life outcomes of the millions of people in extreme poverty worldwide, or a teacher who uses his role within an educational context not simply to reproduce the dynamics of the broader society but to challenge them. Doing so requires them to walk a delicate balance between thoughtful critique and the kind of critique than enables inaction.

Individuals Can (and Cannot) Make a Difference

If there is one particular ethos students come to poverty action with, it is the idea that one person can make a difference. The sentiment behind this is, of course, sound; it is what makes intervening in something as overwhelming as global poverty seem even the smallest bit possible. However, as the shepherds of these students—who are being educated in the United States in elite universities—we as teachers must never lose sight of the fact that they are being fed a constant and heavy dose of the American exceptionalism discussed earlier in the chapter. The tension is that, while we want students to know that they have a responsibility to be engaged in this work and that their individual contributions are valued, we must constantly remind them that not even the most talented, most thoughtful person can, alone, bring about the change that is necessary, because there is nothing "natural" about the existence of poverty. It is created, fashioned out of a global economic arrangement that prioritizes the lives of some at the direct expense of the lives of others. The effort of individuals is critical in challenging that reality, and individuals can have an enormous impact on the lives of others. However, deep societal change will not be effected just because there are enough of the right people working on the right issues— it is not a question of quantity but rather a question of leveraging power to challenge the structures of power that make and keep people poor.

Almost universally, immediate service provision that can be carried out by the individual is more rewarding than the long, hard, and often isolating work that is involved in enacting structural change. One of the consistent challenges that arises in helping students navigate this tension is that students often craft a sort of quantitative calculation that leads them to believe that "enough" service work somehow accumulates into structural change. One student, Amanda, worked in a preschool literacy program teaching four-year-olds from low-income families the basics of literacy and reading. In a classroom exercise that asked students to consider where their work was located on a spectrum, from service provision to structural change, Amanda did not hesitate to place her work on the "structural change" pole of the spectrum. She argued that her work was, indeed, tackling structural issues of poverty because, by providing quality preschool education to these children, the organization was helping lay the groundwork for them to succeed in school and therefore break the cycle of poverty by getting an education. Challenging her idea required her to investigate *why* people are in poverty, examine the relationship(s) between poverty and education, and imagine what the educational system would look like if it were set up to meet the needs of the marginalized members of society. In this conversation, Amanda came to terms with the reality that, though she may be altering the structure of the lives of her students by providing early literacy education (and even this is a stretch because it assumes that what happens in the classroom is powerful enough to push back against the tide of poverty), true structural change operates on a broader level and targets change in the institutions that govern and shape the lives of the poor. On the other hand, Amanda's classmate Raul, who worked as a community organizer with a grassroots community-based organization fighting for tenet rights, admitted to me that sometimes he did not feel like he was doing poverty action work, but activism. His conception of poverty action was service provision, not building power in marginalized communities.

The disconnect between the two students' attitudes about their work is telling, and it speaks to the larger disconnect in the way that young people see (and fail to see) a connection between social movements, poverty action, and civil rights. A component of engaging students in real work on the ground (and not just engaging in the ideas) is helping them disaggregate the concept of "the poor"—enabling them to see individual people with individual stories and circumstances that are forged through a particular material reality. At the same time, we need our students to see these individual stories and people and understand that there is no way to divorce the individual instances, the individual stories, and the individual people from the systemic and institutional conditions that shape their lives. We need them to see the individuals, but we also need to ensure that this vista does not obscure their view of the system.

TEACHING POVERTY: THE POLITICS OF HOPE

We conclude this book with a chapter about "teaching" poverty and reflecting on the educative processes connected to poverty action because it was the navigation of the complexities of teaching a new generation of "poverty actors" that provided the impetus for writing this book and developing the Global Poverty and Practice Minor at UC Berkeley. In this chapter, we have discussed how students often come to the topic of poverty action with a budding sense of injustice, guided by a hope that things can be different, that another world is indeed possible. However, that hope can be dangerous. This is an issue I take up in the #GlobalPOV video *Will Hope End Inequality?*

The #GlobalPOV Project, *"Will Hope End Inequality?"*
www.youtube.com/watch?v=KmtfIWLvt_Q

In recent years, scholars concerned with the alleviation of global poverty have begun to situate hope as an antipoverty intervention. Esther Duflo, a world-renowned economist and the director of the Poverty Action Lab at MIT, is known for making critical interventions and questioning the conventional wisdom that underlies poverty interventions. In a 2013 interview, Duflo (2013) spoke about the importance of hope in poverty action: "Part of the problem for the poor is their perspective on what's possible. Sometimes the rational response may be to hold back and not to try. . . . Giving people opportunities, for themselves or for their children, so they can aspire to something different can start a virtuous circle." This isn't a new idea. We've long known, for example, that the intergenerational transfer of poverty is a process constituted both of material factors, such as debt, and of less quantifiable markers, such the cumulative strain of surviving daily poverty. However, the implications of what Duflo is saying are potentially dangerous and connected to the politics of hope. If the poor's inability to envision change is an important spoke in the ever-moving wheel of poverty, then is their *inability* to aspire, to hope, a part of the poverty "problem"?

But hope isn't capital. It doesn't fill an empty belly, make poisoned fields fertile again, or challenge the international mutual dependency between the global South and the global North. A critical engagement in the power (and limitations) of hope requires an understanding that there are different kinds of hope—not all hope is the same. There is a hope that gives us permission to sit back and wait. It's a hope of complacency—it admits that these problems are too big for us to change and surmises that we are doing all we can. Then there is a hope that makes us grasp onto the things that nobody can take from us. It is the kind of hope that disenfranchised people use as a powerful weapon. It is bold and confrontational, and it is rooted in collective action. It is a hope that reminds us, as Frederick Douglass (1985, 204) did, that "power concedes nothing without a demand." It is a hope that pushes us to demand rather than to accept.

In his article *Hope and Democracy*, Arjun Appadurai (2007, 30) describes hope as an ethical and political principle: "The link of hope to mass politics is a response to the realization that democracy without full popular participation is a new form of oligarchy." Hope is powerful, then, when it's harnessed as an expression of collective rage and collective voice. Educational researcher Jeff Duncan-Andrade (2009, 191) differentiates between different kinds of hope: "Hokey hope would have us believe that change won't cost us anything. This kind of false hope is mendacious. It never acknowledges pain. Audacious hope stares down the painful path and despite the overwhelming odds of us making it down that path to change, we make the journey again and again. There is no other choice." Hope is useful when it compels us to act, not when it gives us permission to do nothing. We need hope, but we need a particular kind of hope—a hope that's grounded in an analysis of structures of power *as* structures of power, a hope that pushes us outward, in community with one another, to fight for change.

What is at stake with this praxis-based pedagogy is the ability to think historically about where the moment we are currently in is rooted historically and, thus, about where we are headed. The young people who fill our classrooms have grown up in the age of neoliberalism. As such, they have made meaning of their lives and the world around them within a certain set of conceptual frameworks, understandings, and ideas that lead them to believe that problems like poverty and racism can be ended. They came of age under the United State's first Black president and the ridiculous, ahistorical notion that we live in a post-racial society. They have answered the mandate to "make poverty history." The making of poverty action and the making of poverty actors in this moment is rooted in these conceptual frameworks and, when not harnessed in a critical manner, it lends itself to a recycling of the same old international do-gooding that emerged from a tradition of development and intervention that is steeped in white supremacist, Americanist, elitist ideology. Hope is not a lazy act; hope should not allow for complacency. Hope should be active. Hope costs. And, in the words of Duncan-Andrade, there is no other choice.

There is another lesson here, which is about the value of being unsettled. Prioritizing angst and discomfort is a key part of how we will get there, by centering the paradoxes and contradictions endemic in global poverty action. The active hope we are interested in relies on an unsettling, an angst. Not an angst that allows us to navel gaze, but an angst that makes it impossible to sit still and do nothing. This is, in many ways, a neoliberal plotline. Although they may not be aware of it, our students are characters in a play; they are on a stage, and in their position on that stage they have the ability to change the story.

We spend a lot of time bemoaning and wringing our hands about the future of higher education. But we act like this future is something that will happen to us, something over which we have no control. What if we were to approach this same sinking feeling in our stomachs with clear eyes and clear heads and make the decision that we are going to play a role in this future? We are not speaking in hyperbole, and we are not speaking in abstract about investing in some sort of mythical future that we will pass on to our children either. We are speaking of making the decision that the future of higher education is determined now. This struggle, one launched from the contradictory and conflicted space of the neoliberal university, is embedded in the creation of its own trajectories of praxis and hope, and it is critical to the project of the (re)making of higher education.

Since the age of development emerged after World War II, the issue of poverty has been categorized under the banner of development. What if we shift these conceptual designations? What if we place poverty in a different category—that of anticolonial struggles, civil rights campaigns, and grassroots efforts to bring about social change? What if we stop considering the "poor" as deficient, deprived bodies that have not yet been incorporated into modern development and instead think of them as those bodies that were captured, bound, and sold; bought, relocated, and buried? What if, rather than seeing the "poor" as outside of the project of development, we acknowledge that they are a product of these very modes of intervention? What if we understand the poor as the revolutionary subject—not the disenfranchised in need of intervention and help, but the marginalized and oppressed poised to make history? When we see the poor in this way, we see poverty action in a particular way, and in that reconceptualization of poverty action, there is no space for help, only space for solidarity.

As we consider the narratives, reflect on the emergence of ideas that emerge from student engagement in poverty action work, and consider the potentially transformative power and danger of the stories that emerge from this work, it is important to root our discussions of these stories in a material context. Many scholars have done work on counter-storytelling and the importance of disrupting the master narrative that weaves a certain story about poverty, poor people, and poverty actors. However, it is important to remember the starting point of this conversation. What we are striving to achieve is not just a disruption of the master narrative but a disruption of a kind of poverty action that is about feeling good and keeping everything exactly the same. We must disrupt the politics of benevolence that position the poverty actor as the savior and the impoverished as the lucky recipients of their charitable deeds. We must train young, enthusiastic people to be hopeful but realistic, self-reflective but not self-absorbed, and imbued with a sense of responsibility but not an inflated ego.

The challenge for us, then, is to think about how we can prepare a team of poverty actors who will disrupt the old, problematic dynamics of poverty interventions, privilege, and power and who will envision and execute a new kind of poverty politics that focuses on the development of solidarities, not aid, and promotes an honest engagement with the dynamics of power, privilege, and responsibility that come along with this work. This is not a task that can be taken lightly, and we are not the only ones engaged in this effort. However, it is necessary that we understand the magnitude of this task if we are to take seriously the questions of how we craft a distinct kind of poverty action pedagogy that takes responsibility for the flawed models that exist as a part of the trajectory from which it emerges.

In this sense, the work we are preparing our students for is the fight against power. This conceptualization sees poverty as an outgrowth of (neo)colonial histories and therefore places poverty action in the lineage of anticolonial and civil rights struggles. Poverty action, then, can be regarded as the unfinished work of civil rights and decolonization. We are therefore preparing our students not simply to develop an ethical framework within which to enter the field of inquiry but to inherit a legacy, to recognize the giants on whose shoulders they stand, and to acknowledge the profound responsibility they have not just to make a difference but to upset the global order that renders some lives more valuable than others.

Acknowledgments

This book emerges out of the Global Poverty and Practice Minor at the University of California, Berkeley. We thank our colleagues in the program and in the related academic units of the Blum Center for Developing Economies and International and Area Studies. In writing the book, we have enjoyed the opportunity to transform individual teaching experiences and discipline-based scholarship into a collective project. This project is not solely ours, and we wish to acknowledge the many other faculty members who are a key presence in the program, including Syed Imran Ali, Sean Burns, Khalid Kadir, Cecilia Lucas, and the members of the Global Poverty and Practice Education Committee. However, the work of the program, and of this book, does not lie solely in the classroom. We have relied heavily on Chetan Chowdhry, our program advisor, to foreground and navigate the ethical dilemmas that accompany global practice. Research assistance for this book was provided by Emma Shaw Crane while she was a research fellow at the Blum Center. Abby VanMuijen's brilliant visual imagination enlivens this book and helped create the #GlobalPOV videos that accompany it. The idea for the book came from Naomi Schneider at UC Press. We are grateful to her and to Kim Robinson for their enthusiastic support of our efforts to contribute to the field of critical poverty studies. Naomi shepherded the various iterations of our manuscript through a rigorous but immensely useful review process. We extend thanks to the reviewers, who generously engaged with our work and whose comments challenged us to more boldly state its purpose and scope.

This book is dedicated to the students at the University of California, Berkeley, whom we have had the privilege to teach and mentor. Their commitment to social justice has inspired this book. In turn, we hope that it will inspire them to continue the difficult work of thinking and acting in an unequal world.

References

Abramovitz, Mimi. 2001. "Everyone Is Still on Welfare: The Role of Redistribution in Social Policy." *Social Work* 46 (4): 297–308.

Abu-Lughod, Lila. 2010. "Against Universals: The Dialects of (Women's) Human Rights and Human Capabilities." In *Rethinking the Human*, edited by M. Molina and D. K. Swearer, 69–94. Cambridge, MA: Harvard University Press.

Acemoglu, Daron, and James A. Robinson. 2012. *Why Nations Fail: The Origins of Power, Prosperity, and Poverty*. New York: Crown Business.

Adams, Vincanne. 2013. *Markets of Sorrow, Labors of Faith: New Orleans in the Wake of Katrina*. Durham: Duke University Press.

Adams, Vincanne, Taslim Van Hattum, and Diana English. 2009. "Chronic Disaster Syndrome: Displacement, Disaster Capitalism, and the Eviction of the Poor from New Orleans." *American Ethnologist* 36 (4): 615–636.

Alexander, Brenna. 2014. "Here versus There: Reflections of a Voluntourist." *San Francisco Chronicle*, June 13. www.sfgate.com/opinion/article/Here-versus-there-Reflections-from-a-5551343.php.

Alinsky, Saul D. 1965. "The War on Poverty: Political Pornography." *The Journal of Social Issues* 21 (1): 40–47.

Andersen, Kurt. 2011. "Person of the Year 2011: The Protester." *Time*, December 14. http://content.time.com/time/specials/packages/article/0,28804,2101745_2102132,00.html.

Appadurai, Arjun. 1990. "Difference and Disjuncture in the Global Cultural Economy." *Theory, Culture and Society* 7 (2): 295–310.

———. 2002. "Deep Democracy: Urban Governmentality and the Horizon of Politics." *Public Culture* 14: 21–47.

———. 2007. "Hope and Democracy." *Public Culture* 19 (1): 29–34.

Armstrong, David. 2008. "Is Bigger Better?" *Forbes*, May 15. www.forbes.com /forbes/2008/0602/066.html.

Atkin, David. 2013. "Trade, Tastes, and Nutrition in India." *American Economic Review* 103 (5): 1629–1663.

Ayres, Robert. 1983. *Banking on the Poor: The World Bank and World Poverty.* Cambridge, MA: MIT Press for the Overseas Development Council.

Bajaj, Vikesh. 2010. "Sun Co-Founder Uses Capitalism to Help Poor." *New York Times*, October 5. www.nytimes.com/2010/10/06/business/global/06khosla .html?.

Banerjee, Abhijit V. 2005. "'New Development Economics' and the Challenge to Theory." *Economic and Political Weekly* 40 (40): 4340–4344.

Banerjee, Abhijit V., and Esther Duflo. 2011. *Poor Economics: A Radical Rethinking of the Way to Fight Global Poverty.* New York: Public Affairs.

Banerjee, Abhijit V., Esther Duflo, Rachel Glennerster, and Cynthia Kinnan. 2015. "The Miracle of Microfinance? Evidence from a Randomized Evaluation." *American Economic Journal: Applied Economics* 7 (1): 22–53.

Baudelaire, Charles. (1869) 1970. *Paris Spleen.* Translated by L. Varèse. New York: New Directions Books.

Bello, Walden. 2007. "Globalization in Retreat: Capitalist Overstretch, Civil Society and the Crisis of the Globalist Project." *Berkeley Journal of Sociology* (51): 209–220.

Berman, Marshall. 1982. *All That Is Solid Melts into Air: The Experience of Modernity.* New York: Verso.

Besley, Timothy, Jose G. Montalvo, and Marta Reynal-Querol. 2011. "Do Educated Leaders Matter?" *Economic Journal* 121 (554): F205–227.

Besley, Timothy, and Marta Reynal-Querol. 2011. "Do Democracies Select More Educated Leaders?" *American Political Science Review* 105 (3): 552–566.

Bhan, Gautam. 2009. "'This Is No Longer the City I Once Knew': Evictions, the Urban Poor and the Right to the City in Millennial Delhi." *Environment and Urbanization* 21 (1): 127–142.

Bishop, Matthew, and Michael Green. 2008. *Philanthrocapitalism: How the Rich Can Save the World.* New York: Bloomsbury Press.

Biswas, Soutik. 2010. "India's Microfinance Suicide Epidemic." *BBC News*, December 16. www.bbc.co.uk/news/world-south-asia-11997571.

Bousquet, Marc. 2008. *How the University Works: Higher Education and the Low-Wage Nation.* New York: New York University Press.

Brown, Kevin. 2008. "'All They Understand Is Force': Debating Culture in Operation Iraqi Freedom." *American Anthropologist* 110: 443–453.

Brown, Wendy. 2004, "'The Most We Can Hope For . . .': Human Rights and the Politics of Fatalism." *South Atlantic Quarterly* 103 (2): 451–463.

Butt, Leslie. 2002. "The Suffering Stranger: Medical Anthropology and International Morality." *Medical Anthropology* 21 (2): 1–24.

Caldeira, Teresa, and James Holston. 2014. "Participatory Urban Planning in Brazil." *Urban Studies,* March 5. doi:10.1177/0042098014524461.

Casaliggi, Carmen, and Paul March-Russell, eds. 2012. *Legacies of Romanticism: Literature, Culture, Aesthetics.* New York: Routledge.

Casey, Katherine, Rachel Glennerster, and Edward Miguel 2012. "Reshaping Institutions: Evidence on Aid Impacts Using a Preanalysis Plan." Quarterly Journal of Economics 127 (4): 1755–1812.

Castells, Manuel. 2012. *Networks of Outrage and Hope: Social Movements in the Internet Age.* New York: Polity.

Cole, Teju. 2012. "The White Savior Industrial Complex." *The Atlantic,* March 21. www.theatlantic.com/international/archive/2012/03/the-white-savior -industrial-complex/254843/.

Comin, Diego, William Easterly, and Erick Gong. 2010. "Was the Wealth of Nations Determined in 1000 BC?" *American Economic Journal: Macroeconomics* 2 (3): 65–97.

Conley, Timothy G., and Christopher R. Udry. 2010. "Learning about a New Technology: Pineapple in Ghana." *American Economic Review* 100 (1): 35–69.

Corburn, Jason. 2005. *Street Science: Community Knowledge and Environmental Health Justice.* Cambridge, MA: MIT Press.

Davis, Rochelle. 2010. "Culture as a Weapon." *Middle East Report* 255: 8–13.

Deaton, Angus. 2013. *The Great Escape: Health, Wealth, and the Origins of Inequality.* Princeton, NJ: Princeton University Press.

Douglass, Frederick. 1857. *Two Speeches.* Rochester, NY: C. P. Dewey.

———. 1985. *The Frederick Douglass Papers.* Series 1, *Speeches, Debates, and Interviews.* Vol. 3, *1855–63.* Edited by John W. Blassingame. New Haven: Yale University Press.

Du Bois, William E. B. (1903) 1994. *The Souls of Black Folk.* New York: Dover Publications.

Duflo, E. 2013. "Q&A: Can We End Poverty?" *Yale Insights,* January 4. http:// insights.som.yale.edu/insights/can-we-end-poverty.

Duncan-Andrade, Jeff. 2009. "Note to Educators: Hope Required When Growing Roses in Concrete." *Harvard Educational Review* 79 (2): 181–194.

Duraiappah, Anantha. K., Pumulo V. Roddy, and Jo-Ellen Parry. 2005. *Have Participatory Approaches Increased Capabilities?* Winnipeg: International Institute for Sustainable Development. www.iisd.org/publications/have-participatory-approaches-increased-capabilities.

Easterly, William. 2006a. "The Big Push Déjà Vu: A Review of Jeffrey Sachs's 'The End of Poverty: Economic Possibilities for Our Time.'" *Journal of Economic Literature* 44 (1): 96–105.

———. 2006b. *The White Man's Burden: Why the West's Efforts to Aid the Rest Have Done So Much Ill and So Little Good.* New York: Penguin Books.

———. 2007. "The Ideology of Development." *Foreign Policy,* June 11. www .foreignpolicy.com/articles/2007/06/11/the_ideology_of_development.

———. 2010. "Re-Inventing the Wheel." *Foreign Policy,* October 12. www .foreignpolicy.com/articles/2010/10/11/reinventing_the_wheel.

———. 2012. "How I Would Not Lead the World Bank." *Foreign Policy,* March 5. www.foreignpolicy.com/articles/2012/03/05/how_i_would_not_lead_the_ world_bank.

———. 2014. *The Tyranny of Experts: Economists, Dictators, and the Forgotten Rights of the Poor.* New York: Basic Books.

Elyachar, Julia. 2012. "Next Practices: Knowledge, Infrastructure, and Public Goods at the Bottom of the Pyramid." *Public Culture* 24 (1): 109–129.

Escobar, Arturo. 1995. *Encountering Development: The Making and Unmaking of the Third World.* Princeton, NJ: Princeton University Press.

Fanon, Frantz. (1961) 2007. *The Wretched of the Earth.* Translated by Richard Philcox. New York: Grove Press.

Finnemore, Martha. 1997. "Redefining Development at the World Bank." In *International Development and the Social Sciences: Essays on the History and Politics of Knowledge,* edited by Fred Cooper and Randall M. Packard, 203–227. Berkeley: University of California Press.

Fisher, William F. 1997. "Doing Good? The Politics and Antipolitics of NGO Practices." *Annual Review of Anthropology* 26: 439–464.

Focus on the Global South. 2015. "Who We Are." www.focusweb.org/about.

Foucault, Michel. (1969) 2002. *The Archaeology of Knowledge.* Translated by A. M. Sheridan Smith. New York: Routledge.

Frank, Andre Gunder 1966. "The Development of Underdevelopment." *Monthly Review* 18 (4): 17–31.

Fraser, Nancy. 2007. *Justice Interruptus: Critical Reflections on the "Postsocial-ist" Condition.* New York: Routledge.

———. 2010. "Injustice at Intersecting Scales: On 'Social Exclusion' and the 'Global Poor.'" *European Journal of Social Theory* 13: 363–371.

Fraser, Nancy, and Linda Gordon. 1994. "A Genealogy of *Dependency:* Tracing a Keyword of the U.S. Welfare State." *Signs* 19 (2): 309–336.

Freire, Paolo. [1970] 2000. *Pedagogy of the Oppressed.* Translated by Myra Bergman Ramos. New York: Continuum.

Freire, Paolo, and Macedo, Donaldo. 1987. *Literacy: Reading the Word and the World.* Santa Barbara: Praeger.

Fryer, Roland. 2011. "Financial Incentives and Student Achievement: Evidence from Randomized Trials." *Quarterly Journal of Economics* 126 (4):1755–1798.

Fukuda-Parr, Sakiko, ed. 2003. *Human Development Report 2003: Millennium Development Goals: A Compact Among Nations to End Human Poverty.* New York: United Nations Development Programme. www.unic .un.org.pl/hdr/hdr2003/hdr03_complete.pdf

Gabaix, Xavier. 2014. "A Sparsity-Based Model of Bounded Rationality." *Quarterly Journal of Economics* 129 (4): 1661–1710.

Galbraith, John Kenneth. 1958. *The Affluent Society.* New York: Houghton Mifflin Harcourt.

Gates, Bill. 2008. "How to Fix Capitalism." *Time,* July 31, 23–29.

Gibson-Graham, J. K. 2008, 'Diverse Economies: Performative Practices For Other Worlds', *Progress in Human Geography* 32 (5): 613–632.

Gibson-Graham, J. K., Jenny Cameron, and Stephen Healy. 2013. *Take Back the Economy: An Ethical Guide for Transforming our Communities.* Minneapolis: University of Minnesota Press.

Gidwani, Vinay. 2008. *Capital, Interrupted: Agrarian Development and the Politics of Work in India.* Minneapolis: University of Minnesota Press.

Giroux, Henry A. 2010. "Bare Pedagogy and the Scourge of Neoliberalism: Rethinking Higher Education as a Democratic Public Sphere." *Educational Forum* 74 (3): 184–196.

———. 2013. "Public Intellectuals against the Neo-Liberal University." *Truth-Out,* October 29. www.truth-out.org/opinion/item/19654-public-intellectuals-against-the-neoliberal-university.

———. 2014. *Neoliberalism's War on Higher Education.* Chicago: Haymarket Books.Global Citizen. 2015. "The Global Citizen Manifesto." www.globalcitizen.org/en/content/the-global-citizen-manifesto/.

Global Poverty Project. 2013. *The Global Citizen Effect: Impact of the Global Citizen Festival.* www.globalpovertyproject.com/globalcitizen/Impact /TheGlobalCitizenEffect_ImpactReport_2013.pdf

Goldman, Michael. 2005. *Imperial Nature: The World Bank and Struggles for Social Justice in the Age of Globalization.* New Haven: Yale University Press.

Gottesdeiner, Laura. 2013. *A Dream Foreclosed: Black America and the Fight for a Place to Call Home.* New York: Zuccotti Park Press.

Grossman, Lev. 2010. "Person of the Year 2010: Mark Zuckerberg." *Time,* December 15. http://content.time.com/time/specials/packages/article /0,28804,2036683_2037183,00.html.

Grow, Brian, and Keith Epstein. 2007. "The Poverty Business." *Businessweek,* May 20. www.businessweek.com/stories/2007-05-20/the-poverty-business.

Grusky, Sara. 2000. "International Service Learning: A Critical Assessment from an Impassioned Advocate." *American Behavioral Scientist* 43 (5): 858–867.

Hall, Stuart. 1988. *The Hard Road to Renewal: Thatcherism and the Crisis of the Left*. New York: Verso.

Han, Judy. 2015. "Our Past is Your Future: Evangelical Missionaries and Memories of Development." In *Territories of Poverty: Rethinking North and South*, edited by Ananya Roy and Emma Shaw Crane, 176–185. Athens, GA: University of Georgia Press.

Hart, Gillian. 2001. "Development Debates in the 1990s: Culs de Sac and Promising Paths." *Progress in Human Geography* 25 (4): 649–658.

Harvey, David. 2005. *The New Imperialism*. Oxford: Oxford University Press.

———. 2008. "The Right to the City." *New Left Review* 53: 23–40.

Hoff, Karla, and Joseph E. Stiglitz. 2010. "Equilibrium Fictions: A Cognitive Approach to Societal Rigidity." *American Economic Review*, 100 (2): 141–146.

Incite! Women of Color Against Violence. 2007. *The Revolution Will Not Be Funded: Beyond the Non-Profit Industrial Complex*. New York: South End Press.

Kanbur, Ravi, and Andy Sumner. 2012. "Poor Countries or Poor People? Development Assistance and the New Geography of Global Poverty." *Journal of International Development* 24: 686–695.

Kapoor, Ilan. 2004. 'Hyper-Self-Reflexive Development? Spivak on Representing the Third World 'Other.'" *Third World Quarterly* 25 (4): 15–16.

Kascak, Lauren, and Sayantani Dasgupta. 2014. "#Instagramming Africa: The Narcissism of Global Voluntourism." *Pacific Standard*, June 19. www.psmag .com/navigation/business-economics/ instagrammingafrica-narcissism-global-voluntourism-83838/

Katz, Michael. 1986. *In the Shadow of the Poorhouse: A Social History of Welfare in America*. New York: Basic Books.

———. 2015. "What Kind of Problem is Poverty?" In *Territories of Poverty: Rethinking North and South*, edited by Ananya Roy and Emma Shaw Crane, 39–78. Athens, GA: University of Georgia Press.

Klein, Naomi. 2010. *The Shock Doctrine: The Rise of Disaster Capitalism*. New York: Picador.

Kraske, Jochen, William H. Becker, William Diamond, and Louis Galambos. 1996. *Bankers with a Mission: The Presidents of the World Bank, 1946–91*. Oxford: Oxford University Press.

Kuhn, Thomas S. 1962. *The Structure of Scientific Revolutions*. Chicago: University of Chicago Press.

Lawson, Victoria. 2012, "Decentering Poverty Studies: Middle Class Alliances and the Social Construction of Poverty." *Singapore Journal of Tropical Geography* 33 (1): 1–19.

Lawson, Victoria, and Sarah Elwood. 2014. "Encountering Poverty: Space, Class, and Poverty Politics." *Antipode* 46 (1): 209–228.

Lefebvre, Henri. (1974) 1991. *The Production of Space.* Translated by Donald Nicholson-Smith. Malden: Blackwell Publishing.

Leonard, David. 2015. "Remixing the Burden: Kony 2012 and the Wages of Whiteness." *Critical Race and Whiteness Studies* 11 (1). www.acrawsa.org.au /files/ejournalfiles/251Leonard2015111.pdf

Leve, Lauren, and Lamia Karim. 2001. "Introduction Privatizing the State: Ethnography of Development, Transnational Capital, and NGOs." *PoLAR: Political and Legal Anthropology Review* 24 (1): 53–58.

Li, Tania Murray. 2007. *The Will to Improve: Governmentality, Development, and the Practice of Politics.* Durham: Duke University Press.

Lovejoy, Paul. 2014 "African Contributions to Science, Technology and Development." UNESCO Slave Route Project, 1–38. www.unesco.org/new/fileadmin /MULTIMEDIA/HQ/CLT/pdf/P_Lovejoy_African_Contributions_Eng_01 .pdf.

Mackey, John, Rajendra Sisodia, and Bill George. 2013. *Conscious Capitalism: Liberating the Heroic Spirit of Business.* Boston: Harvard Business Review Press.

Maisano, Chris. 2012. "The Soul of Student Debt." *Jacobin* 9. www.jacobinmag .com/2012/12/the-soul-of-student-debt/.

Manski, Charles F. 2013. *Public Policy in an Uncertain World: Analysis and Decisions.* Cambridge, MA: Harvard University Press.

Marx, Karl. 1978. "Theses on Feuerbach." In *The Marx-Engels Reader,* edited by Robert C. Tucker, 143–146. New York: W.W. Norton and Company.

Massey, Doreen. 2007. *World City.* Malden, MA: Polity Press.

McIntosh, Peggy. 1990. "White Privilege: Unpacking the Invisible Knapsack." *Independent School* 49 (2): 31.

Mellor, Anne Kostelanetz. 1988. *Romanticism and Feminism.* Bloomington: Indiana University Press.

Merry, Sally E., and Rachel Stern. 2005. "The Female Inheritance Movement in Hong Kong: Theorizing the Local/Global Interface." *Current Anthropology* 46 (3): 387–409.

Miguel, Edward, Colin Camerer, Katherine Casey, Jessica Cohen, Kevin M. Easterling, Alan Gerber, et al. 2014. "Promoting Transparency in Social Science Research." *Science* 343 (6166): 30–31.

Mitchell, Don, and Nik Heynen. 2009. "The Geography of Survival and the Right to the City: Speculations on Surveillance, Legal Innovation, and the Criminalization of Intervention." *Urban Geography* 13 (2–3): 611–632.

Mitchell, Timothy. 1991. *Colonising Egypt.* Berkeley: University of California Press.

———. 2002. *Rule of Experts: Egypt, Techno-Politics, Modernity.* Berkeley: University of California Press.

Mohan, Giles, and Marcus Power. 2009. "Africa, China, and the 'New' Economic Geography of Development." *Singapore Journal of Tropical Geography* 30: 24–28.

Molyneux, Maxine. 2006. "Mothers at the Service of the New Poverty Agenda: Progresa/ Oportunidades, Mexico's Conditional Transfer Programme." *Social Policy and Administration* 40 (4): 425–449.

Munk, Nina. 2013. *The Idealist: Jeffrey Sachs and the Quest to End Poverty.* New York: Doubleday.

Newfield, Christopher. 2008. *Unmaking the Public University.* Cambridge, MA: Harvard University Press.

Nussbaum, Martha. 2004. "Mill Between Aristotle and Bentham." *Daedalus* 133 (2): 60–68.

ONE Campaign. "About ONE." Accessed April 4, 2013. www.one.org /international/about/.

Opoku-Agyemang, Kweku. 2015. "Preference Gravitation: A Theory with Evidence from 'Hands-Free' Mobile Survey Micro-Experiments." Working paper, University of California, Berkeley.

Organisation for Economic Co-Operation and Development. 2014. *The New Development Finance Landscape: Emerging and Preliminary Perspectives from the Cases of Ghana, Senegal and Timor-Leste.* Paris. www.oecd.org /dac/aid-architecture/New%20Development%20Finance%20Land-scape%20interim%20report%20February%202014_final_1.pdf.

Osborne, Martin J., and Ariel Rubinstein. 1994. *A Course in Game Theory.* Cambridge, MA: MIT Press.

Paley, Julia. 2001. *Marketing Democracy: Power and Social Movements in Post-Dictatorship Chile.* Berkeley: University of California Press.

Peck, Jamie. 2010. *Constructions of Neoliberal Reason.* Oxford: Oxford University Press.

Peck, Jamie, and Nik Theodore. 2015. "Paying for Good Behavior: Cash Transfer Policies in the Wild." In *Territories of Poverty: Rethinking North and South,* edited by Ananya Roy and Emma Shaw Crane, 103–125. Athens: University of Georgia Press.

Pew Research Center. 2012. *Fewer, Poorer, Gloomier: The Lost Decade of the American Middle Class.* www.pewsocialtrends.org/2012/08/22/the-lost-decade-of-the-middle-class/

Pieterse, Jan Nederveen. 2000. "After Post-Development." *Third World Quarterly* 21 (2): 175–191.

———. 2011. "Global Rebalancing: Crisis and the East-South Turn." *Development and Change* 42 (1): 22–48.

Piketty, Thomas. 2014. *Capital in the Twenty-First Century.* Translated by A. Goldhammer. Cambridge, MA: Harvard University Press.

Piketty, Thomas, and Emmanuel Saez. 2003. "Income Inequality in the United States, 1913–1998." *Quarterly Journal of Economics* 118 (1): 1–39.

Pithouse, Richard. 2014. "An Urban Commons? Notes from South Africa." In *Commons Sense New Thinking about an Old Idea,* supplement, *Community Development Journal* 49 (S1): i31-i43.

Piven, Frances Fox, and Richard Cloward. 1977. *Poor People's Movements: Why They Succeed, How They Fail.* New York: Pantheon Books.

Polanyi, Karl. (1944) 2001. *The Great Transformation: The Political and Economic Origins of Our Time.* Boston: Beacon Press.

Prahalad, C. K. 2004. *The Fortune at the Bottom of the Pyramid: Eradicating Poverty through Profits.* Cambridge, MA: Wharton School Publishing.

Prashad, Vijay. 2012. *The Poorer Nations: A Possible History of the Global South.* New York: Verso.

Pritchett, Lant. 2013. "Extreme Poverty Is Too Extreme." *Global Development: Views from the Center,* October 7. www.cgdev.org/blog/extreme-poverty-too-extreme.

Rabinow, Paul. 2004. "Midst Anthropology's Problems." In *Global Assemblages: Technology, Politics, and Ethics as Anthropological Problems,* edited by Aihwa Ong and Stephen Collier, 40–55. Malden: Blackwell Publishing.

Raj, Shannon. 2011. "Blood Electronics: Congo's Conflict Minerals and the Legislation that Could Cleanse the Trade." *Southern California Law Review* 94 (981): 981–1034.

Ravallion, Martin. 1994. *Poverty Comparisons.* Chur: Harwood Academic Press.

Rich, Adrienne. 2002. *The Fact of a Doorframe: Poems 1950-2001.* New York: Norton.

———. 1984. *Blood, Bread, and Poetry: Selected Prose, 1979-1985.* London: Little Brown and Co.

Rich, Bruce. 2002. "The World under James Wolfensohn." In *Reinventing the World Bank,* edited by Jonathan Pincus and Jeffrey Winters, 26–53. Ithaca: Cornell University Press.

Riley, Jonathan. 1988. *Liberal Utilitarianism: Social Choice Theory and J.S. Mill's Philosophy.* Cambridge, UK: Cambridge University Press.

Roosevelt, Franklin D. "State of the Union Message to Congress." January 11, 1944. Franklin D. Roosevelt Presidential Library and Museum. www.fdrlibrary.marist.edu/archives/address_text.html.

Rose, Nikolas. 2000. "Community, Citizenship and the Third Way." *American Behavioral Scientist* 43: 1395–1411.

Rosenberger, Cynthia. 2000. "Beyond Empathy: Developing Critical Consciousness through Service Learning." In *Integrating Service Learning and Multicultural Education in Colleges and Universities,* edited by C. O'Grady, 23–44. New York: Routledge.

Roy, Ananya. 2010. *Poverty Capital: Microfinance and the Making of Development*. New York: Routledge.

———. 2011. "The Blockade of the World-Class City: Dialectical Images of Indian Urbanism." In *Worlding Cities: Asian Experiments and the Art of Being Global*, edited by Ananya Roy and Aihwa Ong, 259–278. Chichester: Wiley-Blackwell.

———. 2014. "Slum-Free Cities of the Asian Century: Postcolonial Government and the Project of Inclusive Growth." *Singapore Journal of Tropical Geography* 35: 136–150.

Roy, Ananya, Wendy Larner, and Jamie Peck. 2012. "Book Review Symposium: Jamie Peck's Constructions of Neoliberal Reason." *Progress in Human Geography* 36 (2): 273–281.

Roy, Arundhati. 2001. "The Greater Common Good." In *The Algebra of Infinite Justice*, 43–142. New Delhi: Penguin Books.

Sachs, Jeffrey. 2005. *The End of Poverty: Economic Possibilities for Our Time*. New York: Penguin Press.

———. 2012. "How I Would Lead the World Bank as President." *Washington Post*, March 1. www.washingtonpost.com/opinions/how-i-would-lead-the-world-bank/2012/03/01/gIQAfGbZlR_story.html.

Saez, Emmanuel. 2013. "Striking it Richer: The Evolution of Top Incomes in the United States (Updated with 2013 Preliminary Estimates)." Department of Economics, University of California, Berkeley. http://eml.berkeley.edu/~saez/saez-UStopincomes-2013.pdf.

Sandefur, Justin. 2013. "Africans Care about Jobs; Non-Africans Care about Institutions?" *CSAE Blog*, March 19. http://blogs.csae.ox.ac.uk/2013/03/africans-care-about-jobs-non-africans-care-about-institutions/.

Schultz, Theodore William. (1964) 1976. *Transforming Traditional Agriculture*. New Haven: Yale University Press, 1964. New York: Arno Press.

Schwietert, Julie. 2008. "Top 16 Volunteer Experiences in New Orleans." *Matador Network*. www.matadornetwork.com/change/top-6-volunteer-experiences-in-new-orleans/.

Sen, Amartya. 1970. "The Impossibility of a Paretian Liberal." *Journal of Political Economy* 78 (1): 152–157.

———. 1999. *Development as Freedom*. New York: Oxford University Press.

———. 2006. "The Man Without A Plan" *Foreign Affairs* 85 (2): 171–178. www.foreignaffairs.com/articles/61525/amartya-sen/the-man-without-a-plan.

Sheffield, Carie. 2014. "Deducting Your Mortgage Does Not Make You a Welfare Queen." *Forbes*, February 25. http://www.forbes.com/sites/carriesheffield/2014/02/25/deducting-your-mortgage-does-not-make-you-a-welfare-queen/.

Sheppard, Eric. 2011. "Geography, Nature, and the Question of Development." *Dialogues in Human Geography* 1 (1): 46–75.

Slaughter, Sheila, and Larry L. Leslie. 1997. *Academic Capitalism: Politics, Policies and the Entrepreneurial University*. Baltimore: John Hopkins University Press.

Smith, Neil. 2006. "There's No Such Thing as a Natural Disaster." Understanding Katrina: Perspectives from the Social Sciences, June 11. http://understandingkatrina.ssrc.org/Smith/.

Soley, Lawrence. 1995. *Leasing the Ivory Tower: The Corporate Takeover of Academia*. Boston: South End Press.

Spivak, Gayatri C. 1990. "The Post-Modern Condition: The End of Politics?" In *The Post-Colonial Critic: Interviews, Strategies, Dialogues*, edited by S. Harasym, 17–34. New York: Routledge.

Standing, Guy. 2014. *A Precariat Charter: From Denizens to Citizens*. New York: Bloomsbury Academic.

Stiglitz, Joseph E. 1999. "The World Bank at the Millennium." *Economic Journal* 109 (459): F577–F597.

———. 2002. *Globalization and Its Discontents*. New York: W.W. Norton and Company.

Stiglitz, Joseph E., and Andrew Weiss. 1981. "Credit Rationing in Markets with Imperfect Information." *American Economic Review* 71 (3): 393–410.

Subcomandante Marcos. 2000. "Do Not Forget Ideas Are Also Weapons." *Le Monde Diplomatique*, October. http://mondediplo.com/2000/10/13marcos

Sumner, Andy. 2013. "Poverty, Politics and Aid: Is a Reframing of Global Poverty Approaching?" *Third World Quarterly* 34 (3): 357–377.

Talwalker, Clare. 2012. "What Kind of Global Citizen is the Student Volunteer?" *Journal of Global Citizenship & Equity Education* 2 (2): 21–40.

Taylor, Charles. 1979. *Hegel and Modern Society*. Cambridge, UK: Cambridge University Press.

Thurow, Roger, and Scott Kilman. 2014. *Enough: Why the World's Poor Starve in an Age of Plenty*. New York: PublicAffairs.

Wacquant, Loïc. 2009. *Punishing the Poor: The Neoliberal Government of Social Insecurity*. Durham: Duke University Press.

Walker-Rodriguez, Amanda, and Rodney Hill. 2010. "Human Sex Trafficking." *FBI Law Enforcement Bulletin* 80 (3): 1–8. https://leb.fbi.gov/2011/march/human-sex-trafficking.

Warner, Judith. 2010. "The Charitable Giving Divide." *New York Times*, August 20. www.nytimes.com/2010/08/22/magazine/22FOB-wwln-t.html.

Washburn, Jennifer. 2005. *University, Inc.: The Corporate Corruption of American Higher Education*. New York: Basic Books.

Weeks, Kathi. 2011. *The Problem with Work: Feminism, Marxism, Antiwork Politics, and Postwork Imaginaries*. Durham: Duke University Press.

Weinstein, David. 2007. *Utilitarianism and the New Liberalism*. Cambridge, UK: Cambridge University Press.

Williams, Raymond. 1978. *Marxism and Literature*. Oxford: Oxford University Press.

Wolfensohn, James. 2005. *Voices for the World's Poor: Selected Speeches and Writings of World Bank President James D. Wolfensohn 1995–2005*. Washington, DC: World Bank.

World Bank. 2015. *World Development Report 2015: Mind, Society, and Behavior*. Washington DC: World Bank.

Wright, Erik Olin. 2010. *Envisioning Real Utopias*. London: Verso.

Wyly, Elvin, Markus Moos, Holly Foxcroft, and Emmanuel Kabahizi. 2008. "Subprime Mortgage Segmentation in the American Urban System." *Tijdschrift voor Economische en Sociale Geografie* 99 (1): 3–23.

Zhong, Raymond. 2014. "New Poverty Formula Proves Test for India." *Wall Street Journal*, July 27. www.wsj.com/articles/new-poverty-formula-proves-test-for-india-1406487289.

Ziolkowski, Theodore. 1992. *German Romanticism and Its Institutions*. Princeton, NJ: Princeton University Press.

Index

Page numbers in italic refer to illustrations.